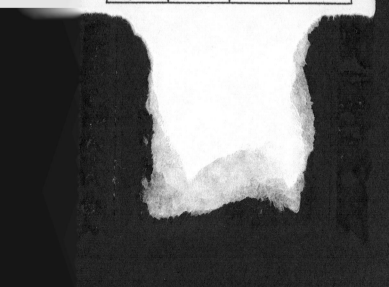

Twayne's United States Authors Series

Sylvia E. Bowman, *Editor*

INDIANA UNIVERSITY

Van Wyck Brooks

VAN WYCK BROOKS

By JAMES R. VITELLI

Lafayette College

(TUSAS) 134

Twayne Publishers, Inc.   ::   New York

MANUFACTURED IN THE UNITED STATES OF AMERICA BY
UNITED PRINTING SERVICES, INC.
NEW HAVEN, CONN.

TO TINKER

Preface

FOR MORE than half a century Van Wyck Brooks was a wholly dedicated partisan for the cause of American literature. Literature for him was never a mere pastime, a business, an adornment, or "something to go in for"; it was life itself, life at its greatest intensity. Writers, the aristocrats of the world, were the leaders, the very makers, of civilization. Without writers and artists passionately committed to a vision of the beautiful, the good, and the true, life simply held no promise of fulfillment.

Van Wyck Brooks arrived at this romantic allegiance very early, and he never got over it. His career was one long sustained attempt to realize a community of art and letters working and located at the very heart of American civilization. During his lifetime American literature came of age, and it did so to the accompaniment of his voice exhorting writers to meet their responsibility with courage and dignity—and with pride in their membership in a great community. He was that literature's herald and guide, and he became its conscience. He provoked and entered one literary battle after another, compelling writers to examine the choices they had made and to confront the problems peculiar to them as Americans. No assessment of the American literary achievement of the past sixty years can be complete, therefore, without recognition of Van Wyck Brooks's role in creating intellectual conditions which in large measure made that achievement possible.

His literary career clearly divides into two major phases. In the first, 1908 to 1927, he devoted himself to an analysis and exposure of the dangerous split in America between literature and life, enforcing his argument with two major emblematic demonstrations of the thwarted careers and talents that resulted. *America's Coming-of-Age* (1915), with its companion volume, *Letters and Leadership* (1918), stirred the generation of writers Brooks first addressed. His account of the division in the American mentality between "highbrow" and "lowbrow" asserted a peculiar force and claim upon the imagination and ambitions of young writers. *The Ordeal of Mark Twain* (1920) and *The Pilgrimage of Henry James* (1925) both sparked controversies and compelled writers to look about them to find where their true resources of artistic strength lay; each was directed at contemporary writers to encourage them neither to yield to lowbrow pressures nor to seek escape in the various refuges of the highbrow. This first phase in Brooks's career ended in his unsuccessful attempt to suggest that a model resolution of the American writer's dilemma might be found in the story of the life of Emerson.

The latter part of his career, commencing in 1932 with his recovery after several years of nervous collapse, was devoted to the task he had consistently called for in his earlier work: the creation of a living tradition, of a "usable past" that would give writers not only assurance of the close ties between literature and life but the sense that they were part of a long lineage. *Makers and Finders: A History of the Writer in America,* written over a period of twenty years, *is* this second phase; moreover, this work is the major achievement of his career. Other works followed, mellower in tone, reminiscent and defensive; but each was part of his effort in this second phase to show that the two countries of the literary artist—the one he lived in and the one in which his imagination had its home—were one and virtually the same.

In my attempt to unfold the pattern and meaning in Brooks's career and work I have proceeded from two assumptions: (1) that the best way to understand Van Wyck Brooks is to treat him as first of all an artist, and (2) that the course of his career with its apparent shifts makes sense and reveals a consistency of aim and purpose only when placed in the context of the changing critical scene and literary situations.

In terms of the first assumption, we can read Van Wyck Brooks on other writers and on the American scene as we have learned to read, say, Henry James on other writers. When Henry James writes about Hawthorne, he does so with an eye to his own predicament as a writer—with awareness of his own ambitions and hopes for the course American literature will take. Similarly, when Van Wyck Brooks writes on Mark Twain, Henry James, Ralph Waldo Emerson, and all the others, he is viewing the predicament of the American writer in the 1920's, the 1930's, and so on—of Van Wyck Brooks first, and of others as represented in him. This first assumption also means that we pay heed to the form and shape of Brooks's work, to the elements of his style, to the imagery, metaphor, and symbol that reveal an essentially creative imagination in charge.

The second assumption ought not to need any explanation; but, since only a few critics have pointed to the inner consistency in Brooks's work through both phases, the purpose of that assumption needs to be underscored. Brooks applied his creative imagination in the broad preserves of literary criticism, and this application involved him necessarily in controversy. A battle of books, as Irving Howe has reminded us, is really one over different styles of life; and from first to last, Brooks fought for a democratic style of life in letters. He firmly hitched his romantic hopes to the prophetic vision of Jefferson, Emerson, and Whitman—a tradition which has always had its ups and downs. The two phases of his career, however, were neither inconsistent nor contradictory; they complemented each other. The shifts were not Brooks's so much as those of the literary periods he lived through.

Critics will continue to be divided in their estimates of Brooks as they divide in their attitudes toward the democratic style and tradition that he championed. But they cannot applaud the historic role he performed in his earlier phase and also dismiss the creative achievement of his later years, for both phases form an entity. He must be judged, finally, by his best works; these, through the creative myth they contain, have had the power to awaken the readers and the makers of books and to goad them into reconsidering the quality of the American literary experience.

I am greatly indebted to a number of people for this study. First of all, to Van Wyck Brooks who first tolerated my queries as far back as 1951 and remained patient thereafter in my repeated attempts to learn more from him. Gladys Brooks extended that courtesy, permitting me access to Van Wyck Brooks's study and leaving me to work there undisturbed over the files put at my disposal.

For encouragement and wise criticism in my developing interests in Brooks and his times, I am especially indebted to Professor Robert E. Spiller. For their patient reading and criticism of my manuscript in its various stages, I am grateful to Professors William W. Watt, William A. Thomas, George P. Winston, Foster Provost, John F. Mahoney, and Derrick Plant.

Also for their criticism, and for various other reasons important to me, I owe thanks to Mr. James R. Blackwood, Mr. James B. Allardice and Alice Allardice, Mr. Robert S. Ricksecker and Jean Ricksecker, and Mr. Edward Breisacher. To Professor Sylvia Bowman, I owe many thanks not only for sound editorial counsel, and for her patience with me, but especially for the rescue and nursing of my manuscript while I was absent for a year in India. The dedication acknowledges my greatest debt. The faults are solely my responsibility.

JAMES R. VITELLI

Lafayette College
Easton, Pennsylvania
January 23, 1967

Acknowledgments

For permission to quote many passages from Van Wyck Brooks's work I am very grateful to Gladys Brooks and to Van Wyck Brooks's American and British publishers as follows:

To J. M. Dent & Sons, Ltd., London publishers of *New England: Indian Summer; The Confident Years: 1885-1915; Opinions of Oliver Allston; Helen Keller: Sketch for a Portrait; Days of the Phoenix: The Nineteen-Twenties I Remember; Scenes and Portraits: Memories of Childhood and Youth; The Dream of Arcadia: American Writers and Artists in Italy, 1760-1915;* and *Howells: His Life and World.* To E. P. Dutton, American publishers of all the above and also the following: *The Ordeal of Mark Twain; The Pilgrimage of Henry James; The Life of Emerson; Three Essays on America* (for all matter from *America's Coming-of-Age, Letters and Leadership* and "The Literary Life in America"); *The Flowering of New England; On Literature Today; The World of Washington Irving; The Times of Melville and Whitman; The Writer in America; From the Shadow of the Mountain: My Post-Meridian Years.* To the University of Pennsylvania Press, publishers of *The Malady of the Ideal.* To Gladys Brooks for permission to quote from *The Wine of the Puritans; The Soul: An Essay Towards a Point of View; John Addington Symonds: A Biographical Study;* and *The World of H. G. Wells.*

I also wish to thank Gladys Brooks for permission to quote letters to and from Van Wyck Brooks, and for permitting me to examine Brooks's early Journal and manuscripts and notes prior to their being deposited with the Library at the University of Pennsylvania. I am grateful to Mrs. Neda Westlake, Curator, Rare Book Collection of the Library, University of Pennsylvania, for extending permission to me to quote from materials now on deposit there, and for a number of courtesies before and since in my uses of the Library's Brooks collection.

Contents

Chronology

1886   Van Wyck Brooks born in Plainfield, New Jersey, February 16, the younger of two sons of Charles Edward Brooks, a stockbroker, and Sarah Bailey (Ames) Brooks.

1891   Entered Plainfield public schools; proved to be a precocious student.

1898   Spent the year with his family in Germany, France, Italy, and England.

1904   Entered Harvard University with the class of 1908, following Maxwell Perkins, his childhood friend from Plainfield. Met John Hall Wheelock and other "literary" students.

1905   Privately printed, with John Hall Wheelock, *Verses by Two Undergraduates.* Became an editor of the *Harvard Advocate.*

1907   Elected to Phi Beta Kappa and granted his Bachelor of Arts degree a year ahead of his class. Sailed for England, alone.

1908   In England, wrote for London journals. Completed his first book of criticism, *The Wine of the Puritans;* published in London in fall; in New York, following spring.

1909   Back in the United States, worked on the *Standard Dictionary* and *Collier's Encyclopaedia;* under Walter H. Page, for the magazine *World's Work;* interviewed and wrote about writers, among them, William Dean Howells. Roomed on W. 23rd St., New York City, frequented Petitpas' and met John Butler Yeats and other artists and writers.

1911   Went to Carmel, California. On April 26 married Eleanor Kenyon Stimson of Plainfield. (By that marriage became the father of two sons, Charles Van Wyck and Oliver Kenyon.) Wrote and had privately printed in San Francisco, *The Soul: An Essay Towards a Point of View,* dedicated to his friend John Butler Yeats.

In the fall became an instructor in English at Leland Stanford University. During two years there commenced writing biographies of John Addington Symonds and H. G. Wells, and critical studies of French writers Henri Frédéric Amiel, Étienne Pivert de Sénancour, and Maurice de Guérin.

1913 Alfred Zimmern, a Fellow of New College, Oxford, invited Brooks to England to teach in the Workers' Educational Association at South Norwood; Brooks lived at Richmond, on the Isle of Wight, and for a year at Kent. Had published in London, in a small edition of two hundred copies, *The Malady of the Ideal*. Commenced writing *America's Coming-of-Age*.

1914 Returned to America after outbreak of war in Europe. *John Addington Symonds* published in New York. Worked for the Century Company, translating from the French, among others, some novels of Romain Rolland. Lived for a winter in Plainfield, then moved to New York City.

1915 Met Randolph Bourne and saw much of him until Bourne's death in December, 1918. *The World of H. G. Wells* published; then *America's Coming-of-Age*.

1917 Became associate editor of the *Seven Arts,* along with Waldo Frank, James Oppenheim, and Paul Rosenfeld.

1918 *Letters and Leadership.* "On Creating a Usable Past" in the *Dial* (April). Revisited Carmel; completed there a book on Mark Twain.

1920. *The Ordeal of Mark Twain.* Settled in Westport, Connecticut. Became literary editor for Alfred Jay Nock's weekly, the *Freeman*. Wrote column "A Reviewer's Notebook" and other essays and reviews until magazine's demise in 1924.

1922 Contributed "The Literary Life in America" for Harold Stearns's *Civilization in the United States*.

1924 Received the Dial Award for 1923. Reader for Harcourt, Brace & Co.

1925 *The Pilgrimage of Henry James.* Commenced study of Emerson.

1927   Edited with Lewis Mumford, Paul Rosenfeld, and Alfred Kreymborg, *The American Caravan.* Suffered nervous breakdown; spent next four years in various places, including England, in search of psychological treatment for what Dr. Carl Jung diagnosed as "chronic melancholia." Wife and friends arranged publication of *Emerson and Others.*

1932   Restored to health; returned to Westport. Collected and published old *Freeman* essays in *Sketches in Criticism. The Life of Emerson.*

1933   Revised edition of *The Ordeal of Mark Twain.*

1934   Published *Three Essays on America*—slightly revised collection of *America's Coming-of-Age, Letters and Leadership,* and "The Literary Life in America."

1935   Elected to the National Council of The League of American Writers.

1936   *The Flowering of New England* awarded Pulitzer Prize for History.

1937   Elected to the American Academy of Arts and Letters, the centenary year of William Dean Howells, the Academy's first president.

1939   Resigned from the League of American Writers.

1940   *New England: Indian Summer, 1865-1915.* Delivered speech, "On Literature Today," at inauguration of Dr. George N. Shuster as President of Hunter College, in New York City, October 10. Moved to Weston, Connecticut.

1941   Became contributing editor for the *New Republic* (until January, 1945). *Opinions of Oliver Allston* (which appeared in serial form, February to August) published in October.

1944   *The World of Washington Irving.*

1946   In March awarded the Gold Medal of the National Institute of Arts and Letters. In August, Eleanor, his wife, died. Moved to New York City with the John Hall Wheelocks.

1947   Married, June 2, to Gladys Rice. *The Times of Melville and Whitman.*

1949   Settled in Bridgewater, Connecticut.

1952   *The Confident Years, 1885-1915*—the final volume in the series, *Makers and Finders: A History of the Writer in America.* Traveled to Ireland.

1953   *The Writer in America.*

1954   *Scenes and Portraits: Memories of Childhood and Youth,* first volume of memoirs.

1955   Traveled to California. *John Sloan: A Painter's Life.*

1956   Spent April and May in Rome, Italy, preparing study of American writers and artists in Italy (*The Dream of Arcadia*). *Helen Keller: Sketch for a Portrait.*

1957   *Days of the Phoenix: The Nineteen Twenties I Remember,* second volume of memoirs.

1958   *From a Writer's Notebook; The Dream of Arcadia: American Writers and Artists in Italy, 1760-1915.*

1959   Traveled to England and Scotland. *Howells: His Life and World.*

1961   *From the Shadow of the Mountain: My Post-Meridian Years,* third and final volume of memoirs.

1962   *Fenollosa and His Circle.* Suffered a stroke late in the summer.

1963   After a period of declining health, died May 2, in Bridgewater, Connecticut.

Van Wyck Brooks

CHAPTER *1*

Early Life and Literary Influences

THE LIFE STORY of a man of letters as a critic is intimately related to the whole literary history of his time. His story is part of a larger one—that of his generation, of its antecedents, of its followers. The usual biographical facts are more often the facts of literary history rather than those of literary biography. The significant biographical facts of Van Wyck Brooks's career are very much a part of the literary history of America since the turn of the century—since American literature's coming of age.

In important ways Brooks figured in the years of rebellion and experiment and high promise that preceded World War I. His biography, first of all, is closely connected with the literary history of the 1910's and early 1920's and with the literary group of those decades: critics like Irving Babbitt, Paul Elmer More, Stuart Sherman, H. L. Mencken, Randolph Bourne, Walter Lippmann, Waldo Frank, and writers like Theodore Dreiser, Sherwood Anderson, Eugene O'Neill, John Dos Passos, Sinclair Lewis, Floyd Dell, Edwin Arlington Robinson, Robert Frost, William Carlos Williams, T. S. Eliot. Brooks is also related, although more obliquely, to those who followed and who extended the collective achievement of these writers.

As a fashioner and explicator, the critic, unlike the poet or novelist, must heed the changing literary fashions of the present. His literary biography is necessarily more complex, for its way is charted not solely over the great circle route of an artist's vision, but through the narrows and inland waters where critical battles are fought. Brooks took both routes: he maintained a steady course in pursuit of his vision of a democratic style in letters, and he defended that style against specific hazards as he saw them—Puritanism, commercialism and the acquisitive spirit, expatriatism, estheticism, "coterie literature," and a host of other issues which have marked the history of literary thought in America ever since the last days of innocence before World War I.

I *A Double World*

The special quality of Brooks's point of view as a critic had its origin in the place and time of his birth in Plainfield, New Jersey, February 16, 1886. Although close to New York City and a Wall Street suburb where brokers and merchants retired at day's end, Plainfield was a sheltered place in a sheltered age. In his memoirs, Brooks recalled the contradiction between the prevailing manners—the "fable agreed upon"—and the quietly despairing private lives within outwardly tranquil dwellings; between the dramatic events "of that savage and lawless epoch of American finance" that transpired in those same homes and on Wall Street and that created frenetic, rapid change in the outer world, and the conspiracy of silence about money, or the expressed scorn for it, that was a mark of the prevailing sense of security and trust in an eternal unchanging order.[1] Later when Brooks wrote of his early years, the memory of these contrasts was still sharp and clear, although colored over with amusement at his younger self. But to the "hyperaesthetic" youth who spent his early childhood and boyhood in such a Plainfield, the sharpness of the contrasts proved disturbing. Very early they made him aware of the doubleness of the world that Americans inhabited.

The sense of a secure world had strong roots. Of "old American stock," his forebears, Dutch and English in origin, can be traced at least to the period of the American Revolution. Both his grandfathers, who were from Vermont, moved to New York to try their fortunes in the city, arriving about the same time as Horace Greeley. Both of them prospered and married New York wives—one of those tracing her parentage to the founder of Plattsburg in upper New York State. The New York influence was the stronger, Brooks recalled, since his grandfathers became so absorbed in the atmosphere of the metropolis that the New England influences in his background were lost. Surrounded in his boyhood with "Plattsburg spoils, old Canton china, Duncan Phyfe chairs and engravings of Trumbull and West," he felt strongly the connections between himself and a solid, though remote, world—an older agrarian order that was "more normal for Americans than the world of trade."

Brooks's early education was in the Plainfield schools, in the years 1897-1904; but by far the most significant of these years was the one spent in Europe, 1898-1899, the first of many European tours for him. There Brooks's family traveled as a matter of course, and only partly to look after his father's business interests, for "Europe" was to most eastern Americans both a natural fever in itself and a recommended cure for every other kind of fever. For Brooks, Europe was "a realm of magic, permanently fixed, secure and solid as the Alps, regrettable in some ways, perhaps, but inviolate and sempiternal." Although questionable in some respects, in its morals and politics, the Continent was looked upon as "a paradise of culture that had scarcely known a beginning and would never know an end."

He spent the year moving from city to city—Antwerp, Brussels, Dresden, Vienna, Rome, Florence, Naples, Paris, and London—visiting the art galleries most of the time. He maintained a journal—eight "volumes" by journey's end, each a little notebook. In a precise boyish script he recorded his enthusiasms and his disappointments—his tentative first ventures into criticism. In Dresden at the Zwinger Gallery his "mind first came to life," and about the same time he also read Mrs. Anna Brownell Jameson's *Italian Painters*. The two experiences started him, he said, on a course of reading that "determined the main tenor" of his life. Mrs. Jameson's book—a popular handbook for English-speaking tourists of Europe's art galleries—led him in turn to John Ruskin.

From Ruskin, above all, he acquired his ambition to become a critic, a strange ambition for a young boy to seize upon—strange, that is, until that *fin de siècle* mood is recalled, until one remembers the Utopian impulse in Ruskin and how his notions of art and economics appealed to many young minds of the day. But to Brooks it was the *total* experience that counted, not merely his mind's discovery of Ruskin. The journal he kept reveals a sensitive nature, capable of responding not only to the color and forms of art inside the galleries but also to the sensuous atmosphere of the life outside. Italy, especially, appealed to him, and thereafter always remained important, providing him with a kind of standard against which he tested the cultural environment of America. While he was in fact surrounded by the centuries, reading art histories and absorbing Ruskin, Brooks's whole being came alive to a sense of the past in the stream of the present. Before he knew what "tradition" was, he had felt it; and this early experience of it subsequently drove him to look for something like it in America.

Then too there were highly impressionable Henry James-like encounters with other personalities abroad. He met Arthur Ryder, later renowned as a translator and Sanskrit scholar, who became something of a youthful uncle or older brother to Brooks. Brooks remembered him as broadly learned and sweetly disdainful of anything but the life of art and the mind. On a later trip to Italy, the summer after his freshman year at Harvard, he met "another sort of mentor": G. E. Marshall, an Englishman, one of those types of professional tutors in Italy such as may still be met there, who also scorned "the machinery of life." Each left his mark on Brooks by confirming his readings in Ruskin; each helped express for him his own distaste for "efficiency" and the "strenuous life."

Following this exposure to a solid sense of order in an older past, the young awakened mind recoiled from the imitation world in Plainfield. Its artifacts and representatives of culture were but pale copies and timid reminders of Europe. There was even an art gallery, hung with fourth-rate academy pictures, and most of the Plainfield houses had on their walls "dusky copies of Raphael madonnas or Ribera monks, Murillo beggar-boys or Caravaggio gamblers"—just enough, in short, to tease and provoke the newly dedicated art critic and to fire in him a determination to return to Europe.

There were other influences in Plainfield which also inclined Brooks toward his career as a writer. Several "literary people" were there from time to time. Julian Hawthorne, the son of the great romancer and a popular novelist himself, was one of them. Edmund Clarence Stedman, who had spent part of his youth in Plainfield, illustrated how a man might succeed both on Wall Street and as a poet. A critic and essayist of some note, Stedman had performed valuable service in measuring the rank and worth of American poets, being among the first to call attention to the greatness of Emily Dickinson and Walt Whitman. Nearby lived Bret Harte's wife and daughter. The spirit of Washington Irving was active everywhere—sustained in the Dutch names of many townspeople. For Brooks, Irving seemed still alive; his grandmother had once met the distinguished writer and spoke of him as a still living presence. With Maxwell Perkins, his close boyhood friend, Brooks shared an easy familiarity with the world of arts and letters. The Perkins family, New Englanders of Boston and New Haven, could count in its circle of friends men like Charles Eliot Norton and W. W. Story. Later, when Max Perkins and Brooks were at Harvard together, Grandmother Perkins gave the boys for their literary club letters from some old friends of the Perkins clan in Italy and Boston—Robert Browning, Henry W. Longfellow, James Russell Lowell, and John Lothrop Motley among them.

This pleasant brownstone world had its unsettling features, however. Brooks's father, like his mother, was solidly Episcopalian, a Republican, and the embodiment in many ways of a life supposedly resting on permanent laws. But Brooks knew his father only as a semi-invalid. In a town whose quiet homes may have hidden as many as fifty millionaires—presidents of New York banks or Western railroads, heads of mining companies and corporations—the Brooks family could never be said to have had "money" in their neighbors' sense of the word. "We were supposed to be poor, more or less," he recalled; and that fact was part of the disquieting feeling that underlay these early years, otherwise apparently serene.

His father, competing with millionaires in Wall Street, was not cut out to survive. Financial failure always threatened, and sudden misfortunes of neighbors—from overspeculation or, worse, from the exposure of their sins of embezzlement—were not infrequent. The "National Nickel Company," the name on the door of his father's office in Nassau Street, grew more and more fictitious; and the burdens of financing distant and unprofitable mines wore his father to a shadow. Young Brooks, student of Ruskin and sensitive to hints of disaster in the family's outwardly secure life, reacted strongly against the whole mess of the "business life": he grew to hate it. To him, genteel poverty was distasteful, hypocritical.

II *Influences at Harvard*

Since the mores and pressures of tradition insisted that sacrifices be made, there was enough money to insure a university education for Brooks and his older brother, Charles Ames. For the first son, it was Princeton, following a New Jersey custom. For Van Wyck Brooks, possibly because his friend Max Perkins had preceded him there by a year, it was Harvard, which he entered in 1904. In a sense, it seemed inevitable that he should go to Harvard, for by then he already knew that he "was a writer born," and where else but to Harvard did writers go?

Brooks was graduated, Phi Beta Kappa, in 1907, a year ahead of his classmates. The years were few, but filled with experiences. The literary atmosphere especially was heavy. From the first he found his "natural level," for he was introduced by Max Perkins to the "right" people and to the "literary men" among his contemporaries. He joined a literary club, The Stylus, and the staff of the *Harvard Advocate,* of which he became an editor.

The earlier years of travel in Europe proved only too good a preparation for Harvard, for it then "looked backward in time and across the sea." There was a general feeling that the present was unlovely, even degenerate; a mild atmosphere of estheticism carried over from the 1890's still prevailed. It was fashionable to deplore the vulgarities of America and to echo Matthew Arnold's still recent verdict of its dullness. To compensate, young estheticism found sweet excitement in a cultivated sadness for things lost and gone (except, of course, at Harvard) and in various worshipful gestures toward Europe and the past. Brooks shared these reactions and attitudes.

Harvard personalities lent weight and dignity to many of the attitudes that were to characterize Harvard graduates in those years—"neither American nor European." Not least among these influences were the still felt presences of the celebrities of a few decades earlier, kept alive by Charles Eliot Norton, who was the confidant of Emerson, Thomas Carlyle, Ruskin, and Lowell, and who still held open house for students for readings of Dante. Brooks attended two such Sunday "Dante evenings," following the text of the *Paradiso* "while Norton read aloud, like a learned, elegant and venerable priest dispensing sacred mysteries to a circle of heretics, perhaps, who were unworthy of them." There was "something sacramental, even," Brooks reminisced, "in the sherry and the caraway cakes that a maidservant placed in our hands as we were about to depart."

George Santayana, also at Harvard, was completing his volumes on *The Life of Reason.* His velvet-sheathed ironies, so often directed at the frosty Puritan sensibilities of New England, delighted undergraduates, Brooks among them. Brooks admired the style and, more than he admitted in subsequent years, shared many of Santayana's attitudes toward the genteel culture which was officially in charge at Harvard. Perhaps, even, it was at Harvard, and from Santayana, that Brooks first caught a glimpse of the two mentalities that divided America.

It was the mentality of the genteel tradition, however, that reigned at Harvard. The other, that of aggressive enterprise, lay hidden at home in a Wall Street suburb. At Harvard, Professor Barrett Wendell, granting a special dispensation to New England, deplored the rest of the American scene and found the modern writers altogether distasteful. Irving Babbitt, frustrated in his wish to teach the classics, repulsed the esthetic Brooks. Babbitt's "grunts, blowings and gurgitations, roaring his opponents down, harsh and abrupt in manner and voice," were too much at odds with that philosophy of humanism, of decorum and restraint which Babbitt counseled as the only antidote to the evils of the present. But Brooks learned much from Babbitt; perhaps he was more in his debt than to any other single professor encountered at Harvard.

Both teacher and student, ironically, published a first book of criticism in the same year, 1908. Babbitt's *Literature and the American College* was published after a decade of patient, cautious work in the academic vineyards. Brooks's *The Wine of the Puritans,* a work of precocity and daring, appeared within a year of his departure from Harvard. Each book subsequently proved to have been the opening shot for each side in the main critical debate of the next two decades.

Because Babbitt and Brooks were the leaders of the opposing critical camps, and because Brooks repeatedly censured the barbaric personality and manners of Babbitt, the similarity of the critical points of view of both men has been obscured. Babbitt's dogmatic attack upon modernism violated the inner natures of many of his students who shared Brooks's romantic sensibilities and who, like Brooks, reacted strongly. But their dispute with Babbitt over the romantic ego further obscured, perhaps from Brooks himself, the more profound ways in which the teacher influenced the student.

Babbitt's way of looking at literature, for instance, became in many respects Brooks's. Babbitt was interested above all in literary ideas, with their tendencies, with the way they moved from one writer to another, from one literary period to another, and with the way these ideas reflected a style of life and influenced a way of living. He steadily disavowed any intention of "rounded estimates" of writers or their work; instead, he concentrated on the movement of literary forces in reaction or revolt from a desirable norm for both literature and life—a norm he defined as humanism. Moreover, Babbitt stretched his web of analysis over a framework of critical ideas, chiefly the ideas of eighteenth- and nineteenth-century French critics.

Brooks, for his part, had been inclined with something like dedication toward both criticism and French culture even before he met Babbitt in the classroom. In his first year abroad he began the lifelong devotion to the literature and language of the French that resulted in over thirty translations and in consistent reliance upon the dicta of writers like Henri Amiel, Ernest Renan, and Charles Sainte-Beuve. If there were no meeting of harmonious temperaments, both Brooks and Babbitt had minds with the same slant. Most of all, it was Babbitt's point of departure, the examining of literary ideas within a patterned figure of history, which Brooks learned from him at Harvard.

Other influences at Harvard, as it appeared to him in retrospect, moved his sensibilities rather than his intellect. His professors and his fellow students did not form him into the kind of writer he was to be so much as confirm him in his belief that he must be one. Since nearly everyone at Harvard wrote books, the assumption was that all would—or so it seemed to Brooks. Accordingly, in 1905, before he had left Harvard yard, Brooks published his first book, a thin pamphlet, *Verses by Two Undergraduates*. John Hall Wheelock, destined to be his lifelong and most devoted friend, was the other undergraduate who contributed half of the twenty poems, one to a page. Brooks's poems graced the right-hand pages, and Wheelock's the left-hand (though the anonymity of the pamphlet's title was preserved throughout). Although this book was Brooks's first, it was of less consequence to him than to his friend Wheelock who went on to achieve considerable reputation as a poet.

Brooks succeeded in keeping copies of this first youthful venture well hidden,[2] though he need not have been so modest. The poems are imitative, as might be expected, and scented with the esthetic airs of the time. But they are delicately and skillfully written, and they show, for a pair of undergraduates, considerable mastery of the conventional forms. One could not have predicted which poet held the greater promise.

Others at Harvard in these years touched Brooks only lightly or not at all. Yet mention of only a few names suggests how much the literary storms of the next several years began to gather there. For instance, during Brooks's undergraduate years Stuart Sherman was in the graduate school and was becoming a disciple of Babbitt. Not far behind Brooks were T. S. Eliot (1910), also listening closely to Babbitt, and Conrad Aiken (1911), both becoming, like Brooks, editors of the *Harvard Advocate*. (Eliot in fact wrote the *Advocate's* review of Brooks's *The Wine of the Puritans*, finding it "a wholesome revelation.")

On the faculty, among the professors of literature, there were—besides Babbitt and Barrett Wendell—George Lyman Kittredge and George P. Baker, who arrived with his "47 Workshop" (1905-1925) about the time Brooks did. The nearly legendary Professor Copeland, with whom Brooks said he "somehow never hit it off," and Bliss Perry, who combined for a while his professorship in English with his duties as editor of the *Atlantic Monthly*, were also on the faculty. The elective system gave Brooks the chance to hear them, as well as Henry James, who visited Cambridge in 1905 to lecture on Balzac, and James Bryce, the astute British observer of the American Commonwealth. Brooks's literary interests were counterbalanced by little else, though he "listened" to the history lectures of Professor Haskins and to the philosophies of Professor Hugo Munsterberg and Josiah Royce. Curiously, he altogether missed William James and did not discover his affinity for "this enemy of all despair" until after his Harvard years.

III *The Appeal of Europe*

Inevitable as it had been for Brooks to go to Harvard, it seemed equally inevitable that, scarcely a month out of college, he should head once again for Europe—this time, however, to England and on his own. But while he was still at Harvard he had made a gesture at starting a writing career of some kind in New York City. A letter from Irving Babbitt had taken him to Paul Elmer More, then an editor of the New York *Evening Post*, a goal for aspiring writers. More gave him a book to review and then furnished him with still another letter, introducing him as coming "from Harvard with the intention of taking up literary work."[3] Brooks used the letter to gain entrance into other literary offices in New York. More's phrase "taking up literary work" settled in his mind to signify for him, later, a particular attitude of Americans toward literature as something, like stocks and bonds, to "take up." Just before his departure for Europe he had even dared to lay siege to William Dean Howells, then residing at a hotel in New York, to seek advice about how to become a writer.

The sympathy and guidance Brooks received from his peers at home, however, were nothing compared with the appeal of Europe. At Harvard, Brooks and Max Perkins had come to know Frederick Moore, already a seasoned correspondent and author who had come from Britain to study for a year at Cambridge under Professor Charles Townsend Copeland. Visibly embodying Fleet Street journalism, a Richard Harding Davis type, Moore was more attractive to Brooks than Howells. Moreover, Moore's invitation to Brooks and his friends, promising introductions to London editors, was not to be denied.

At home, Brooks's father had died, and his mother willingly conspired to forward her son's interests. Perhaps, too, another attraction from across the sea was the presence in Paris of Eleanor Kenyon Stimson, the girl he was to marry a few years later in 1911. She had recently joined her brother who was studying architecture at the Beaux Arts in Paris. So, in the summer of 1907, Brooks crossed the Atlantic, traveling steerage. He endured this meanness and that of the area around Soho where he settled because he was romantically "pleased with poverty" and had a "sentimental reverence for sordid things."

The eighteen months that followed were ones of apprenticeship at the craft of writing. They were also months when the earlier youthful ambition to become an art critic or an art historian underwent modification. Assisted by Frederick Moore's letters of introduction, he was shortly at work in a literary agency where he clipped stories from English newspapers to be sent to America and rewrote European articles "in American style." Later, profiting by commissions secured for him by Moore, he contributed columns to a Manchester newspaper and wrote with the authority of a native American upon subjects like Tammany Hall, Theodore Roosevelt, and William Jennings Bryan. For the *Contemporary Review* he wrote an article on "Harvard and American Life." The drudgery of the job with the literary agency quickly disillusioned him about a life of journalism, but the assignments directed his attention to America. As a result, he who had gone to Europe partly out of revulsion for America and Americanism found the lines of force attracting him back. Closely examining his own desires, his position as an American abroad, and the similar position of so many of his friends scattered all over Europe, he began to feel that his real theme was "America and Art"—not merely "Art."

He wanted, moreover, to write a book, not just an article or two. Again Frederick Moore came to his assistance with encouragement and, more important, a quiet farmhouse residence in Sussex in West Chiltington near Pulborough. There, in February, 1908, Brooks withdrew from London journalism to spend the next four months writing *The Wine of the Puritans: A Study of Present Day America,* which was published in London the following fall.

IV *Apprenticeship in New York City*

From that point on, the significant biography of Van Wyck Brooks as an American critic is largely the story of his books and of how they relate to the literary history of his times. Other important influences, of course, touched him in the years that followed and contributed to his growth as a writer and to his ability as a critic. But the three areas of experience in his formative years—Plainfield, Harvard, Europe—remained the controlling ones. These he poured into his first book, and they set him on the course he was to follow as a critic: to reconcile the contradictions within and between each area, to pursue and find for America that sense of tradition which Europe stood for and which Europeans seemed to possess. Moreover *The Wine of the Puritans* itself influenced him, for it committed him to develop his point of view.

What he did thereafter, whom he met, where he lived, and what he read, thought, and felt about, provided evidence that confirmed him in his commitment. These experiences sharpened his dislike of commercialism, renewed his sense of Europe's cultural homogeneity, and deepened his conviction of America's need for tradition. He probed his own instincts and struggled to express them more clearly, vowing in his journal to develop a style that would be "a lesson to Americans." He met artists and writers who shared his feelings, assuring him that he was not alone. He read more widely in American literature, adding to his already prodigious background of reading in Europe's literature. He found some ideas—such as those of psychology—which proved useful for investigating a nation's soul. But none of these new influences in his development altered in any fundamental way the course he had set in *The Wine of the Puritans*.

When he returned to New York early in 1909, he knew what he wanted to do. The first stage of his apprenticeship as a writer was over. The next four years, 1909-1913, found him engaged in an ambitious program of self-improvement, partly in New York City, partly at the other end of the continent in California, and partly in England—for art's sake and for the sake of living. First, in New York, he saw the American edition of *The Wine of the Puritans* through the press with his publisher, Mitchell Kennerley, an enterprising man who dared to publish books by unknown writers. Then Max Perkins, already established at Scribner's, secured a position for Brooks with Doubleday and Page where he assisted the editor, Walter Hines Page, on the magazine *World's Work*.

In the one year of his association with this magazine Brooks wrote of his interviews with several men of letters of the day, among them, Augustus Thomas, whose success on Broadway with *The Witching Hour* (1907) had made him America's leading playwright. For the same purpose Brooks made a return visit to William Dean Howells. The difference between the supplicatory purpose of his first approach to Howells and the published report of his second interview was a measure of the young writer's gain in self-assurance. The words of respect with which Brooks handled his "portrait" did not disguise a note of mild disdain and impatience with all that Howells represented. "There is a tradition that centers in him, and its flavor is native American," he wrote of Howells, but, he added, Howells was "a little too fastidious." True though his novels were to common things, "one rebels against them." The characters in Howells' novels, he complained, all appeared the same size—under middle height.

In a note to Brooks following the appearance of the article, Howells delivered a mild rebuke: "It could only have been better if you had known more of my books."[4] Brooks long afterward amply confessed the truth of the charge and more than atoned for it. He also suggested how much, at the time, Howells had represented everything against which he had rebelled. Brooks had found the metaphor of the Puritan ready at hand for use in his first book, and at least one face of the Puritan—the pale, other-worldly profile—came alive for him in Howells.

The other aspect of the Puritan, of which he had caught bare glimpses in Plainfield, was the aggressive Philistinism of the commercial world. This side he saw all about him in New York where even the magazine and publishing world was dominated by the spirit of business enterprise. At Petitpas', however, a gathering place for writers and artists that suggested the *vie de Bohème*, Brooks found a pleasant mediating ground. Common in the literary and art centers of Europe, such places have been rare in America where "centers" are seldom long-lived enough to acquire the settling strength of a tradition. Petitpas' was a little French restaurant and pension at 317 West 29th Street managed by three sisters.

There another of Brooks's early teachers reigned, a personality that naturally attracted writers and artists around him. John Butler Yeats, father of the poet W. B. Yeats, had arrived in New York in 1908 in his seventieth year, settled there, and lived out his remaining fifteen years with Petitpas' as his headquarters. "A born portrait-painter imprisoned in an imperfect technique" (by his own judgment), Yeats brought with him the flavor and excitement of the literary revival in Ireland. Brooks, with his classmate Edward Sheldon, who was already established as a playwright of some promise, met Yeats early in 1909 and their friendship lasted until the elder man's death in 1921. Yeats sketched several portraits of Brooks, using the pastels he had just taken up after his arrival in America.

At Petitpas', where Brooks went to eat and talk, he found Yeats surrounded by men like Robert Henri, William J. Glackens, John Sloan, the brothers Maurice and Charles Prendergast, and occasionally George Bellows—artists all. Each of them had been rebuffed by the National Academy of Art and, led by Henri, had participated in an independent show of their works that had given them collective notoriety as the "Revolutionary Black Gang," as the "Apostles of Ugliness," and finally as the "Ashcan School" of American painters—a term still used to identify them. With these artists, with the bubbling talk of Yeats and his allusions to the Irish writers—to Æ (George William Russell) and John M. Synge, Lady Augusta Gregory, and the Abbey Theatre

—Brooks considered himself perched on the edge of a revival in America. He felt strongly the role he must play in smoothing out a path for its continuing success.

Yeats's talk settled deeply into Brooks's mind and reappeared later in his books, often in direct quotation but more frequently as a close echo. Brooks wrote about Yeats several times,[5] but the influence of Yeats as an instructor on life and art is detectable throughout his writing. Brooks, for instance, was fond of quoting William Blake's phrase, "Art and science cannot exist but in minutely organized particulars." He often recited these words in defense of his essays in biography—even in as late a work as his biography of Howells. Behind the fondness for this phrase and its purport lay the memory of Yeats's reiterated liking for the concrete and the tangible that were always to be preferred, he had instructed Brooks, to the abstract and the speculative. This preference was for Yeats, as it became for Brooks, an expression of a style of life that was Thoreau-like in its insistence upon confronting the particulars of life, respectful of and awed by the meanest no less than by the greatest. This attitude, which became a working principle for Brooks, was responsible for the virtues of his achievement as well as for its weakness. His critics, of course, did not neglect to point out that Brooks, in emphasizing so many particulars of the literary life in America, too often rendered all the makers of its literature as of the same height—"six feet tall."[6]

The effect of Yeats on Brooks was most apparent, however, during the years of their almost daily meetings with one another. Brooks's animus toward the Puritan-commercial spirit in America and his buoyant optimism about a new day for the arts derived support from the spirited talk led by Yeats at Petitpas'. Brooks had already made the identification between Puritanism and commercialism—it was commonly made, in fact, by the young intellectuals of the day—but Yeats's repeated discourses on the waste of spirit resulting from the pursuit of dollars and the way he insistently coupled this acquisitive impulse with a Puritan-hatred of human nature provided ringing phrases and an attractive, if all too simple, diagnosis of what ailed art in America.

The difference between the broadside scattering of Brooks's shots at Puritanism in *The Wine of the Puritans* and the heuristic formula he tossed at his generation in *America's Coming-of-Age* is one measure of Yeats's influence on him. Another is Yeats's challenge which Brooks quoted in the latter book: "The fiddles are tuning as it were all over America." Yeats's phrase, picked up by his young auditor, announced the high hopes of the prewar literary generation. The connection between the moods of prewar and postwar America—accounting as much as the interruption of World War I for the apparent overnight change from joyous expectation of success to gloomy acceptance of failure, which amounted almost to a cult of failure—lay in the all too successful discovery of the pervading presence in America of the Puritan and the dominance of business enterprise. Brooks's role in developing this critical posture for his literary generation, with its indebtedness to Yeats, is one of the central ironies in his career.

V *Socialism and Young Rebels: Randolph Bourne*

As with his venture into journalism in London, the "hack-work" and the business spirit which governed his assignments in New York could not long hold him against the tugs of his ambition to write books. Besides, there was an affair of the heart to pursue, and the lady was in California. Accordingly, early in 1911 he headed west, had privately printed in San Francisco a forty-page pamphlet, *The Soul: An Essay Towards a Point of View* ("To J. B. Yeats . . . Tu se' lo mio maestro"), married Eleanor Kenyon Stimson in April, and settled for some months at Carmel on the Monterey peninsula. There he prepared for the fall term at Leland Stanford University where he had been engaged as an instructor to teach American literature. In the two years that followed, while keeping one step ahead of his students, he also managed to write parts of three books: *John Addington Symonds: A Biographical Study* and *The World of H. G. Wells,* both published by Mitchell Kennerley, and *The Malady of the Ideal.*

California, especially the Carmel atmosphere, which has influenced writers as diverse as John Steinbeck, Henry Miller, and Robinson Jeffers, had a puzzling attraction for Brooks. He revisited it many times in later years, but these early ones remained the more important, because they passed when he was struggling to define a point of view for himself, when he came studiously to grips with American literature, and when he tried to find, in the contradictory extremes of a Pacific civilization, a clue to the opposing extremes in the country.

His socialism—still a theory derived from Ruskin and characterized by an instinct for humanity rather than by any reasoned political position—met actuality in California but not that of "conditions" which socialism promised to correct; for this experience came later. In California Brooks met other self-styled socialists; for, like the protagonist of Floyd Dell's *Moon Calf*, an archetypal biography of Brooks's generation, Brooks found a flourishing socialist "local" led by immigrant "intellectuals" with minds "full of Karl Marx and Freud, Krafft-Ebing, Nietzsche, Bakunin, Kropotkin." He was drawn into this circle, he wrote later, by a number of motives, but chiefly by the romantic attraction he found in the rebels and revolutionaries associated with all varieties of socialism, with their "interest in ideas where ideas were few."

The socialist impulse drew him back to England in 1913 when he returned with his wife and first son to teach in the Workers' Educational Association. The experience of teaching working men and women—shoemakers, milkmen, boatmakers, mechanics, and potters—and discovering in them a zeal for literature "in and for itself," left a deep impression upon Brooks. His meetings with literary people—like H. G. Wells—who in turn avowed themselves to be socialists, aiming at amelioration of the working man's lot, added another dimension to his thinking about the relation of life and literature in America. "All this," he recalled, "led me to think of the differences between America and England, as it led me to see the good in various conditions of English life that, in one way or another, were different from our own. Its cultural centralization was one of these conditions, the focusing of the general mind so that every English feeling and thought had its instantaneous effect on every other."

Brooks was not alone, nor the first, to experience this sense of unity, centrality, and homogeneity in the fabric of national cultural lives in Europe that so contrasted to the heterogeneous cultures of America and to the disparities between American ideals and practices. What is noteworthy is the number of young men, contemporary with Brooks, who had this experience at about the same time and in the same places, and who returned home determined to find or create a similar world for Americans.

Walter Lippmann, whom Brooks met in England during this second stay, was one; Randolph Bourne, then on his *Wanderjahr* in Europe, another. Within months, just as World War I turned American pilgrims homeward, these men and others like them discovered one another's common feelings and ambitions.

Upon Brooks's return to America, Lippmann invited him to participate in the new weekly which he and Herbert Croly were planning. The *New Republic,* launched in October, 1914, was intended as a kind of actualization of H. G. Wells's *Blue Weekly* in *The New Machiavelli.* Lippmann described it to Brooks as a "weekly of ideas" designed to relate the "noble dream" of America to the "actual limitations of existence." Eventually, Brooks appeared in its columns, as did Randolph Bourne, who became a contributing editor. But the alliance among the younger intelligentsia rested not so much upon common political views as upon their desire to advance America into the mainstream of art and culture. The *Seven Arts* (1916-1917) came closer than the *New Republic* to speaking for the kind of unity the young men felt, just as Brooks's *America's Coming-of-Age* (1915), rather than Lippmann's *Drift and Mastery* (1914), phrased, in terms more congenial to them, their "rebel program."

While in England Brooks wrote and completed (in the spring of 1914) a short book, *America's Coming-of-Age,* which proved to be the manifesto for a new generation of writers—one comparable in effect, as Malcolm Cowley has judged it, to Emerson's *American Scholar* (1837). Though it has been suggested that *America's Coming-of-Age* was "to a large extent inspired by Bourne's crusading fury,"[7] Brooks and Bourne had each coiled his spring separately, largely unaware of the other until their actual meeting in November, 1915. Then occurred the instant recognition of their shared wish to arouse a "new class-consciousness, a sort of offensive and defensive alliance of the younger intelligentsia, and the awakened elements of the labor groups."[8]

For a brief time in the years left to Bourne (he died in December, 1918), the interaction between the two minds was strong. The essays each wrote for the *Seven Arts* were complementary in their aim and in the energy with which each writer tried to break down the barriers to an American cultural renaissance. They differed only in tone: Brooks was more petulant and more insistent; Bourne, while frequently hitting the same notes, preserved more consistently the wry sounds of the ironist writing "above the battle."

How much Bourne influenced Brooks's developing critical position toward America can only be guessed. They were in remarkable agreement, even before they met, on their diagnosis of American cultural inferiority. Their brief but intense years of friendship strengthened their common purpose to lift the American head high with new pride in a new nationalism. Each accepted the other as the natural leader for any program of action they might commonly arrive at. But, while assuming that they both wanted the same thing, Bourne professed puzzlement at how Brooks intended to proceed. At times, Bourne seemed to defer to his friend's leadership, offering assistance if Brooks would only make clearer to him what his program was. At other times he took the lead, instructing Brooks on how they must meet the post-war mood—whose discontent he strikingly anticipated. He sought to persuade Brooks to see the positive achievement of that nineteenth-century American literature that both had been inclined to reject—especially in the thread Bourne saw running through Thoreau, Emerson, Whitman, and William James. In particular, Bourne hoped that Brooks might revise his dark judgments of Mark Twain.

Although there were differences, these were muted by the stronger bond of devotion to the ideal of an organic community of art and life. Whether Bourne might have succeeded in getting Brooks to alter in any important way the thesis he expounded in *The Ordeal of Mark Twain* is doubtful. Actually, Bourne's death may have only darkened the tones and shadows of Brooks's book, and one measure of how the association with Bourne affected Brooks is found in the comparable tones of tragic national and personal loss which he expressed both in writing of Twain and in his 1920 essay on Bourne. There can be little doubt that Bourne's death added to the sense of despair and pessimism which clouded much of Brooks's post-war writing.

On the other hand, the more important measure of Bourne's influence on Brooks is to be found in the way he eventually uncovered and defined an American tradition precisely on that line first proposed by his friend. There were other reasons why Brooks became the advocate of that Emersonian line as *the* American tradition, but the memory of Randolph Bourne served him as a conscience in directing him to it. In the space and devotion given to Bourne in a volume of his *Makers and Finders* (*The Confident Years*), in his memoirs, in the longer, later essay on Bourne (in *Fenollosa and His Circle*, 1962) that is one of the last things he wrote, and in the way he appropriated some of Bourne's central ideas—like "trans-nationalism"—Brooks amply testified to his friend's presence in his own critical development.

War in Europe in 1914, marking the breakdown of that homogeneous culture with which so many young Americans had become enamoured, sent Brooks home again; he did not return to Europe for nearly thirty-five years. In the winter of 1914-1915 he resided in his native Wall Street suburb in Plainfield. He renewed his friendship with Max Perkins and entertained J. B. Yeats when he made portrait-painting visits to the city. He suffered again his distaste for the business world—"the business that was never talked about but that somehow pervaded this native scene." He was struck, he remembered, by "the almost pure 'Anglo-Saxonism' of the world I had grown up in as contrasted with the world I had come to know." So he fled, finally, in 1920, from this "little corner of the country, with windows opening towards Europe and closed towards the West" to Connecticut where, with New York City in easy reach, so many of the new writers gathered.

Brooks had returned from Europe with a sense of accomplishment. He had defined for himself a point of view, and felt that his "own curtain was about to rise, that [his] real life as a writer was about to begin." With the publication of *America's Coming-of-Age* in the year after his return from Europe, others too were compelled to note the appearance of an important American writer. For an understanding of how he gained that recognition one must examine how, in his earlier writing, he defined a point of view for himself, The way that point of view, in turn, engaged him in successive literary battles, and the ways in which he honored his commitment to create a "usable" American literary tradition constitute the significance of Van Wyck Brooks the writer.

CHAPTER 2

A Point of View

IT IS A COMMONPLACE that a writer's first book, especially that of a young novelist, is largely autobiographical. This influence would appear less likely, however, for the writer who has determined upon a career as a critic because the role he has chosen presumably directs his attention to things outside himself. Yet, Van Wyck Brooks's first book of criticism, *The Wine of the Puritans* (1908), was largely a species of self-criticism and was derived from the life he had lived and witnessed, felt and thought about, in Plainfield, at Harvard, and in the art galleries of Europe. Although this brief work came from a half dozen highly impressionable years of an avowed esthete, it also looked ahead, mapping out a program that became, finally, the work of a lifetime. Brooks's high ambition—or pretentiousness, as one reviewer noted, with some justification—was spoken in his subtitle: *A Study of Present-Day America*.

The form in which he cast the final version[1] reveals the autobiographical impulse behind it—a dialogue between Graeling and the anonymous narrator. In part, the dialogue is simply a device for setting up a pattern of questions and answers, for the speakers are so much in harmony and there is so little effort made to distinguish the words of one as he picks up the thread spun by the other that their identities merge. Despite the attempt to preserve the formal appearance of a dialogue, the book is really a kind of interior monologue because there is no clash of opposing opinions, no give and take, no dialectic. Since the questions raised carry their damning answers with them, the whole discourse is rather like that of someone who is rationalizing about his hurt feelings.

It is probably true, as Brooks himself said, that the form of *The Wine of the Puritans* had been shaped by the impression made on him by G. Lowes Dickinson's *A Modern Symposium*. Probably, too, it was a projection of his experience with the fortnightly discussion groups he had participated in at Harvard, where each spokesman assumed the point of view of the poet, the painter, the musician, and so on. Since the dialogue is presented as occurring on a slope overlooking the Bay of Naples— a setting integral with the theme—it was probably also a reshaping and an idealization of his conversations with his English friend, G. E. Marshall, who, like Graeling of *The Wine of the Puritans,* scorned "the machinery of life." When the book is seen, however, as the first of a series of attempts to create a voice for himself, a persona or mask, it then becomes apparent how much of Brooks's criticism, like the works of many a nineteenth-century romanticist, was really a dialogue with himself. He announced in his first book what F. W. Dupee has called "the old subjective ethos of romanticism,"[2] and the questions Brooks raised about America's treatment of art and the artist were the insistences of an inner nature that was groping to realize itself. The choice of the form for the work came in response, therefore, to sources deeper than those he later suggested.

The Wine of the Puritans is an important book not only for what it reveals about the emergence of an important American critic but because of its theme: why is the creative life in America so often abortive? In fact, much of the recent critical discussion about the plight of art in a mass culture is a rehashing. of questions Brooks raised. The book has never been reissued since the few hundred copies of its English and American editions in 1908 and 1909, but it deserves to be.* Despite the disarming naiveté of some of its pages, the simple directness of its two speakers provides a refreshing discovery after the "gobbledygook" about inner and outer directedness, masscult and midcult, that has poured from an army of social and cultural analysts since World War II. Reading *The Wine of the Puritans* today is like sighting the first metaphor before it has aged into cliché.

The book is discursive. Paul Rosenfeld complained that each of its paragraphs "appears to be setting out to traverse the universe by a different route, and to be doing everything but joining in a procession."[3] The form of the dialogue gives some credence

---

* Since this was written it has been reprinted, along with selections from *The Soul,* in *Van Wyck Brooks: The Early Years, A Selection from His Works, 1908-1921,* edited with introduction and notes by Claire Sprague (New York: Harper Torchbooks, Harper & Row, 1968).

to this criticism, of course, yet the book has its unity. Each paragraph is held together by a common metaphor, from which comes the book's title: the figure of old wine in new bottles. From this figure comes the narrative of an America divided between the commercial spirit and a remote, lofty idealism. To state the argument so baldly gives little hint, however, of the quality of the critical voice Brooks created for himself. The thesis comes through, not in reasoned discourse, but through an imaginative exploitation of a melancholy mood.

"How do you suppose it all came about?" is the somewhat abrupt question voiced within a few short paragraphs of the opening, one which sets the scene with quick impressionistic strokes: "It was one of those Italian midsummer afternoons, when to be abroad, they say, is the same thing as to be an American." Some hundred pages later this idea is phrased more explicitly: "The question is, why are *we* abroad—we, I mean, so far as we represent a considerable number? To use the dialect we have taken up, are we not cultivating our distraction from American life rather than our extraction from it?"

In between the reiterated questions, the two speakers have explored the sources of their mood, of their sense of "distraction" from their homeland. They place it, first of all, with the Pilgrim fathers, "the first materialists." They speak then of the continuing dominance of "the native-born Puritan race" with its provincial and material ideas and of the present inadequacy of its ideals: " 'You put the old wine into new bottles,' I suggested, 'and when the explosion results, one may say, the aroma passes into the air and the wine spills on the floor. The aroma, or the ideal, turns into transcendentalism, and the wine, or the real, becomes commercialism. In any case, one doesn't preserve a great deal of well-tempered, genial wine.' "

Thereafter, this image provides the explanation of every contradiction the two speakers can touch upon. The Puritan tradition had inclined Americans toward the material side of life. As one consequence, "American civilization had not yet learned to accept the machinery of life as a premise" and so Americans could not accept "the arts of life." Since Puritanism made for an undue emphasis on the rational approach, Americans had neglected to cultivate the "instincts"; consequently, the American "is independent of tradition" because he insists on thinking things out for himself, not trusting the feelings he has inherited from his "race." The American "race," originating with the Puritans, had never had a "childhood" and had come into being fully grown with no prior life of pure impulse and feeling.

And so the conversation moves, touching upon the consequences and symptoms of the divorce between feeling and intellect in the several areas of American life: in politics, business, education, religion—and especially in language and habits of speech, in humor, and in literature and art. American speech betrayed its people when they spoke of literature and art not as normal experiences but as things to "go in for" or to "blow ourselves to." The literature—the poems of William Cullen Bryant and John Greenleaf Whittier—that might have been adequate for provincial New England was no longer suitable for cosmopolitan America. Moreover, the art revealed no racial background, only a brilliancy of technique.

The tone throughout is essentially urbane, only mildly ironic. There is one crude attempt at satire—in a thrust at Jack London and the "Apoplectic School" of writers. There is one outburst approaching anger, aimed not at American Philistinism but at American idealism: where Americans are idealists they are, by reaction, "such *impossible* idealists!—utterly scorning the real and the useful and the practical." But the book ends on a quietly pronounced hopeful note by predicting the appearance soon of "the first great American satirist" who, along with other "great constructors, great positive forces," will help "bind together the estranged fragments of society."

The argument that everything in America is in a state of distraction and divorce, leading to a distortion of cultural values, Brooks expounded repeatedly thereafter, making it peculiarly his own. A whole generation of young writers echoed him until the argument became commonplace. The image of the Puritan, invoked to convey the thesis and also to account for it, likewise controlled the point of view that Brooks wrote from in all his early writing through his book on Henry James. And as with the argument, following the lead of Brooks, then Bourne, and after them, H. L. Mencken, the young men of the 1910's and 1920's made the Puritan their particular dragon. Perhaps no great satirist appeared—though H. L. Mencken and Sinclair Lewis made good tries—but the voice of the ironist became a dominant one in American criticism, poetry, and fiction, from a Randolph

Bourne's voice to those speaking the portraits of a Prufrock and a Jay Gatsby.

Brooks's argument rested, of course, somewhat perilously on a paradox (which he confessed to in an earlier draft but cut from his final version). At bottom, this same paradox was responsible for much of the irony in American writing of the next two decades and gave rise to the stereotype of the American artist besieged in Philistia. Brooks's book is important, therefore, as a forecast of what soon became a common attitude among writers. He had suggested that, though it was essential for the American artist and man of letters to stay in America, it was nearly impossible for him to do so and remain or become truly an artist. He had urged the need for a native tradition, yet he could point to none in America that was not restrictive of talent or destructive to artistic integrity. Others soon joined him, unmindful of the paradox, and mixed denunciation of their American inheritances with confident prophecy of new beginnings. Some who resigned themselves to the paradox fled America to seek a nourishing tradition elsewhere. But here, at the beginning, Brooks was one of the first of the new writers to confront the American artist's dilemma, to ask whether there was a native tradition, and to insist on the importance of a viable relationship between the individual talent and tradition.

In the same year, 1908, Irving Babbitt's *Literature and the American College* provided the opening statement of the position of the humanists on this question. For Babbitt, most of the modern world was suffering from the excesses of a romantic worshiping of the individual ego. He scorned the consequences of this excess as he found it betrayed in tendencies everywhere in the American college—in the elective system, in the stress placed in writing classes upon self-expression, in the use of "a pedantry of originality" (an excessive striving after novelty and eccentricity in contemporary scholarship), and in the vogue of impressionism. Like Brooks, Babbitt was concerned with suggesting reasons for the confusion of values that each agreed prevailed in the modern world. Unlike Brooks, he placed the blame chiefly on the tendency ever since Rousseau—as Babbitt read the intellectual history of the recent past—for the artist to yield to a sentimental identification of himself with his natural surroundings. Tradition, the humanist one of a bygone classical age, was consequently lost and violated by a procession of vain egos, each making itself its own standard.

Brooks, on the other hand, seems to have had his former teacher in mind when, calling for a positive "constructive force in the present," he complained that the trouble with American attitudes toward tradition "comes from living on the past or rather on reactions from the past—which is negative." Americans, he said, were too self-conscious about tradition. Subsequently, he and Randolph Bourne made it clearer that what they meant was only an undue reverence for an Anglo-Saxon tradition at the expense of native American traditions. This American attitude led to what Bourne called "our cultural humility." What Bourne and Brooks chiefly objected to in Babbitt's formulation of a humanist tradition was that it was a cold intellectual abstraction, something of a fiction, with which an artist could not naturally *feel* himself a part. Americans, Brooks argued in *The Wine of the Puritans,* should simply *be* American; and the tradition that he felt was important was a matter of "racial instinct," something absorbed and felt—a notion that was anathema to Babbitt who scorned it as typically romantic.

Finally, however, the emphasis Brooks placed upon the role of the artist's personality vis-à-vis tradition most clearly placed him at opposite poles from Babbitt. It also foreshadowed his opposition to the critical stand of his younger contemporary, T. S. Eliot, also Irving Babbitt's student and one more profoundly and positively influenced by Babbitt than Brooks. Curiously, Brooks came very close to one aspect of Eliot's thinking about tradition. In "Tradition and the Individual Talent" (1917) Eliot first expressed his now famous definition of the organic nature of tradition: "The existing monuments form an ideal order among themselves, which is modified by the introduction of the new (the really new) work of art among them." This is not very different from Brooks's earlier statement in *The Wine of the Puritans:* "And as for originality, it seems to me that all true originality immediately reconciles itself with tradition, has in itself the elements of tradition, and is really the shadow of tradition thrown across the future."[4]

Although this similar appreciation of tradition as a living thing involving a constant organic adjustment between old and new provides a common point of departure, each critic arrived at a very different end. For Brooks, tradition remained alive only in those artists who "felt" it in their bones, who absorbed American life instinctively. Eliot said flatly, "It [tradition] cannot be inherited, and if you want it you must obtain it by great labour." For Brooks, writing at a time when it seemed no American tradition existed, it was "impossible to train oneself in an American tradition" except possibly to develop "a brilliant technique"— and that was like cultivating "a brilliant complexion without cultivating health." However, the whole tendency of Eliot's essay, in which he developed his "impersonal theory of poetry" (in his analogy of the platinum catalyst and the mind of the poet), suggested that the poet matured precisely as he studiously learned to perfect himself as a medium, refining a technique that, like a catalyst, becomes capable of precipitating a new form or compound. "The point of view which I am struggling to attack," Elliot wrote, "is perhaps related to the metaphysical theory of the substantial unity of the soul: for my meaning is, that the poet has, not a 'personality' to express, but a particular medium. . . ." The artist progressed through "a continual extinction of personality."

The point of view Eliot attacked was exactly that of Brooks, who had written in *The Wine of the Puritans:* " 'A great artist does not merge himself in his subjects, he merges his subjects in himself. His personality is always greater than any single manifestation of it. He has a philosophy, a point of view. . . . He must be something more than he knows. He must have some criterion of instinct to which he submits all aftergrowths of technique and conscious experience.' "

In a curious two-page Appendix Brooks made it quite clear that this point of view was related to a metaphysical theory about the unity of the soul with its surroundings. This passage is quoted from a study of Emerson by Vernon Lee, but phrases were underscored by Brooks to indicate not only his agreement with them but their relevance to his own essay. Most contemporary scholars of Emerson would probably agree that the passage betrays a profound misreading of Emerson's concept of the soul. It suggests that Emerson regarded the soul as "utterly unconnected with the things among which it alights," that he was unaware (as Vernon Lee was, Brooks assenting) that "between the soul and its surroundings there will be a growing relation and harmony. . . ." Unfortunately, Brooks's assumption that he was in disagreement with Emerson illustrates how much his early judgments of nineteenth-century American writers rested on just such secondary comments, and it accounts in part for the delay in his eventual recognition of his closeness to Emerson.

Although neither Brooks nor Eliot can be called metaphysicians, the disagreements that prevailed between them, with Brooks assailing Eliot and his followers as a "coterie" that widened the gap between life and literature, the fundamental source of difference between them and the critical positions they represent is metaphysical. It is no longer fashionable to speak of the "soul," much less of its unity with nature; but that metaphysical concept remains central to Brooks's critical point of view. And this concept in the "ethos of romanticism" provides an inner consistency to all his work.

I *Literature and Personality*

At least two of Brooks's books have been described as prose-poems—*The Malady of the Ideal* and *The Life of Emerson*. And in fact he began, as a young poet is likely to do, in a lyrical mood, speaking the disturbances of his own inner being. *The Soul: An Essay Towards a Point of View* and *The Malady of the Ideal* are two such lyrical expressions, addressed even more than *The Wine of the Puritans* to himself. *The Soul* was privately printed in San Francisco; and except for a few copies he sent his friends (one to Irving Babbitt), Brooks left most of them to be disposed of by the landlady of the flat he vacated when he got married. *The Malady,* printed in London in a very small edition, was hardly known even by his friends, and was practically unavailable until 1947 when Robert E. Spiller persuaded him to issue the first American edition. Both essays are, as Spiller wrote of the latter, "a little like the inspired letter written late at night and torn to fragments in the cool of the morning; . . . valuable to others because it was not meant for them."

The Soul is the more private, the more confessional of the two. The "I" speaks unabashedly its ponderings of the great questions: what is life, what is love, why the great conflict between one's inner world and the outer world, where is truth? Like a young Ben Franklin laying down a regimen for his soul, he vows:

To caress life with its little fragile offerings of light, to reject nothing but the fixed forms of half-truths, to learn without cynicism to see through everything as one sees through a crystal, to be in solution, in perpetual readiness, to be as responsive as mercury, to have instant sympathy with everything in the very moment it comes to our attention, never to think ourselves small because the universe is large, to be conscious of ourselves only in moments of growth, to quit nothing until we have begun to see the nobility in it, to wait and hope and dream until the whole world has become vibrant with sense and the apparency of things has melted away and we see in everything a connection with everything else, meaning within meaning. . . .

But what difficulty confronts the soul in its striving for identification and connection with the infinite—especially in a world in which science had become the criterion of truth! In "the outer world" the intuitive sense of man's identity with nature was hampered "by the mortal dress in which he found himself." In this conflict lay the origin of poetry, the soul's way of seeking consolation for its peculiar dilemma. The tortured soul wants to find love, identity, but it is thwarted by society. "In literature," Brooks confessed, "I seemed to see a refuge"; but literature, like life, also had its conditions. If it were "less than one's whole self," it became cold, hard, unreal—"in a word, rhetoric."[5]

Life opposed to literature, poetry to rhetoric, the soul to society: to reconcile each of these became Brooks's assumed task as a critic; and his aim sprang from a need to accomplish the same reconciliation for himself. But it was first necessary to explore the consequences of these several conflicts, a kind of personal exorcism to shore up his own determination not to succumb to the "malady" of pursuing the ideal. There were dangers, as Brooks knew, in contemplating the soul too directly. In the epigraph to The Malady of the Ideal he warned: "O Psyche! Psyche! preserve thy good fortune; do not sound the mystery too deeply." One way out was to sound the mystery indirectly, through the lives of other artists. Another was to insure the indirection through metaphor and symbol, with the method of the impressionist, and from behind a mask.

II The Malady of the Ideal

In the last analysis, as Robert E. Spiller has said, The Malady of the Ideal is a prose-poem; and its form reveals more the synthesizing mind of the artist at work than the analytical mind of the critic. It takes off on the wings of a metaphor, a typically romantic one that presents the clash between man and nature, each trying to press its sense of order upon the other. At first, the opening passage promises to provide a dramatic setting, as in *The Wine of the Puritans,* and a narrator's voice speaks in the first person plural:

> For a few days we had returned from our wanderings. In the late afternoon we went back to the house we had left at the opening of spring. Still unoccupied, it had kept pace with the inevitable season, and the tangled garden had blossomed into high summer just the same. But how helplessly and in what confusion! The rose-bushes—yellow, white, pink and red—had scrambled into bloom, and the ambitious buds, half-blown and deprived of water, were blasted among the insect-ridden leaves. The crimson fuchsias without assistance were struggling to unroll their purple hearts. The brakes and ferns meanwhile were in a high feather, and the dandelions and a few wild roses had urged themselves riotously among the gentler growths.

This opening device is responsible for setting the confessional tone of what follows, as though all that is said were meant only for the ear of some shadowy alter ego. (Shortly thereafter, however, the narrator's voice becomes single and remains so throughout.) The thesis emerges rather from the image of a garden—man's attempt at imposing order on apparent chaos, but violated by an "exuberant and blind" resurgence of wilderness—"nature's order rather than ours." The moment the narrator perceives this order amid apparent chaos is one of those disinterested moments of intuition and of poetry, "the outer body of intuitions." Like other nineteenth-century American romanticists before him, Brooks asserted that the strife between laws for man and nature's law was only an appearance of man's making; it was the result of his failure to see his own place in the natural order. (Though Brooks did not appreciate it as yet, Emerson had also delighted in using some organic metaphor to proclaim his insight into the harmony between "each and all" of nature's objects. They are, he wrote in *The American Scholar,* not "chaotic, and are not foreign, but have a law which is also a law of the human mind.")

Brooks's opening metaphor—repeated with variations elsewhere in his essay—showed that he had found a metaphysical basis

[*49*]

for his hitherto purely impulsive reaction to the dichotomy of all things American; and, for himself at least, he had formulated an answer to the question he had raised in *The Wine of the Puritans*. Also, as he proceeded to apply this transcendental concept to the three representatives of the French mind and French literature he chose—Étienne de Sénancour, the author of *Obermann;* Maurice de Guérin; and Henri Amiel—he defined his proposed task as a critic.

The romantic soul of the narrator expressed its anguish at the "gigantic fallacy" men subscribed to in their failure to perceive the "federation" that already existed between them and the universe. Mankind, craving for order, "perpetually overreaches itself" and snatches at perversions, Brooks bemoaned through his mask. "The spiritual nature of the individual will never be perfectly free until the collective nature is submerged in an all-embracing routine," he said. But the social order—"patriotism and other forms of what may be called world-pride" (Puritanism was one of these)—demanded its tribute of the inner life, too often committed the human spirit to something fixed and static, and placed it in a position of antagonism "to the order of the universe." Here, still perhaps without fully appreciating it, Brooks sounded very much like Emerson trying to state his concept of the Oversoul, except that these terms were often the same ones with which Brooks subsequently explained his socialism—a twentieth-century overlay on a nineteenth-century idea.

Pursuing an Emersonian correspondence, he noted that literature found itself in the same dilemma as life, confronting us with "an interior order and an exterior order, the former being the apprehension of truth, the latter the form in which the writer seeks to convey it." In literature, too, a fundamental antagonism existed "inasmuch as form implies some outward consistency." When the artist imposed an enforced consistency upon his material, he yielded to the demands of the social or outward order and became a rhetorician. The "true poet," however, "characterized by perfect sincerity, a trait of the inward order," never yielded to outer demands for order—never, that is, was content to *impose* form on his materials. Instead, being true to his inner nature, to his intuitive perception of truth, he constantly reached deeper and deeper into himself, seeking not consistency, not method, but "truth"—his sense of the connectedness of all things, himself among them. Form, in short, for Brooks, was equated with the integrated personality, the whole person, whole because at one with the universal order.

This concept of form as personality is important for defining the kind of literary critic Brooks became, as well as for understanding the several genres his own writing followed. From first to last he concerned himself, as a critic of literature, with the literary personality and with the way the artist achieved fulfillment in his art. That he was not an "esthetic" critic, one concerned with an analysis of the principles operating within the work of art itself, has been the one point of common agreement about him among his critics. He was, however, in accord with most contemporary textual or analytical critics in assuming the organic unity of form and content in works of art, but he was heir to Emerson and Whitman rather than to Samuel Taylor Coleridge in insisting that the test of the unity is found in the personality of the artist and in the way his entire life's work, rather than just the single work, reveals him as either a "rhetorician" or a "true poet."

The identification of form with personality was, in Irving Babbitt's lexicon, a romantic heresy, inviting the overthrow of tradition or any other kind of restraint, discipline, and responsibility. Brooks did, in fact, in *The Malady*, virtually deny that the "true poet" should commit himself to technical considerations of craftsmanship. The well-designed work he suspected as "rhetoric," a "form of infidelity." It was only, he wrote, by a "lack of method that a man achieves in his work the only kind of self-accordance possible in the expression of thought—that which exists in the personality itself, widening, deepening in its perception, but still true to nature because true to itself."

Tradition also stood as an obstacle in the way of the poet; a frozen form that was part of the social order, it imposed restrictive demands upon him. Recoiling from the traditional postures of the social world, finding them abrasive of his talents, Sénancour fell back on the "only touchstone within reach, the sum-total of his own intuitions." The result could be seen in *Obermann*, "the book of a man suspended, waiting," unable to rest on any middle ground between the strictly individual and the strictly universal—unable, finally, to establish identity between the two. Maurice de Guérin, deeply learned in history and philosophy, found the forces of spontaneous creation halted by a "phantom" as soon as an idea possessed him: "it is the image of this idea composed of words." "What passes in the air" affects the repose of his soul, and so he is only the half-artist, incapable of releasing himself fully through traditional forms of thought and language.

The compulsions of tradition cheated Amiel of his destiny too. Though he found his deepest affinities with the ego and subjective mind of German philosophy, he mistakenly felt it his duty to justify himself to his French public and friends. He attempted "a self-development in harmony with French tradition," an attempt that paralyzed the poet in him. The French tongue, the whole Gallic race in his bones, permitted only a stuttering expression of his German soul. His Calvinistic inheritance preached Duty to him, turned him from his poet's role to perform a multitude of microscopic tasks, and tainted his ardor for the ideal self with a suspicion that some worm was after all at the core of Being.

Each poet, as Brooks read his fragmented life and works, had in various ways succumbed before the several tyrannies of tradition. Yet, the need for tradition—felt in one's bones—was important to Brooks too. To resolve the conflicting demands upon him of his inner nature and of the tradition that was a part of his inner being was the dilemma confronting the artist. It was also the dilemma Brooks faced as a critic, but the problem was confounded by his acute sense of the absence of a distinctively American tradition into which he and other Americans could merge themselves and achieve personal fulfillment.

The Malady of the Ideal, and in fact the whole of Brooks's work, is in a special sense as much a work of the creative imagination as it is of critical analysis. It has close affinity to the main body of American literature as that collective achievement has been characterized by the impulse toward self-definition. *The Malady of the Ideal* contains a quest for identity—the fate of those who, compelled to express themselves, are driven into an endless search for the proper form to embody their identity without violating it.

A number of scholars have recently emphasized this theme as one that gives coherence to American literature and the "American experience." One of these, Earl H. Rovit, drawing upon the insights of scholars like H. B. Parkes, R. W. B. Lewis, Richard Chase and others, notes that "in a sense the attempted self and culture definitions of our American writers comprise the totality of American literature," and that these attempts were inevitable results of the American's experience of being thrust "into temporal and spatial isolation without a framework of tradition or society which could give him the security of self-definition."[6] In *The Wine of the Puritans* and *The Malady of the Ideal* Brooks was simultaneously speaking from that experience of metaphysical isolation and addressing himself to it.

In the early phase of his criticism, Brooks was almost obsessively concerned with the plight of the alienated artist. At the same time, feeling a kinship with so many of those he studied, he emulated them in experimenting with form, trying to find the proper angle from which to express his point of view. Rovit has observed, for instance, how often the American fiction writer, trying to find a formal technique for dealing with the demands of defining or integrating "the metaphysically isolate," was forced to invent "some kind of dramatic structure in which his self-definition could be narrated *in time*" and therefore developed a form in which the protagonist becomes "the learner" and the dramatic action is the process through which he learns. Both *The Wine of the Puritans* and *The Malady of the Ideal* are launched upon such a dramatic device, and the "voice" in each is that of a learner. As Rovit also observes, this structural device gradually "splits the traditional protagonist into two characters; the single hero of thought and action becomes double: an observing man of thought and an active participant in life." With Brooks, this doubleness of the critic-protagonist, the creation of a voice for himself, was not merely a structural device; it was also an accurate projection of his dual function as both observer and actor in the American literary scene.

These early works by Brooks were, in short, experimental attempts at symbolic statement of a personal experience—like so much of American literature. The *materials* of that experience were for Brooks largely literary, so he confronted them in the guise of a critic. But his encounters with these materials were so intensely personal that he first had to deal with them after the manner of the artist. The point of view he defined for himself in these early confessional writings was integral with the ways he chose to find it. Having done so, he was prepared to drop his mask and apply his point of view as though it were an analytical instrument.

CHAPTER 3

The Point of View Applied

WHEN Van Wyck Brooks returned to England in 1913, with his wife and young son, he took with him the manuscripts for three books. Before he departed from England the following fall, he had published one of these, *The Malady of the Ideal,* and had written still another. Within a year of his return to America, he had cleaned out his file of manuscripts and had three more published books to his credit. Friendly reviewers began referring to him as "one of the most brilliant of the younger American critics," and hostile reviewers complimented him by singling him out as representative of all the heresies of the younger generation. He enjoyed the distinction of being an acknowledged leader in a full-scale battle of books. The sudden reputation came from the collective impact of the three books which came after *The Malady of the Ideal: John Addington Symonds: A Biographical Study* (1914); *The World of H. G. Wells* (1915); and, above all, *America's Coming-of-Age* (1915).

His first book of criticism, *The Wine of the Puritans,* had brought only modest recognition, generally praiseworthy. As might be expected, British reviewers, since their own sensitivities were not under attack, were favorably impressed; but most American reviewers qualified their appreciation of his style to take issue with the "severity" of his chastisement of America. *The Soul* was not seen by reviewers, and *The Malady of the Ideal* went entirely unnoticed in America and nearly so in England.[1] Yet, without these first three efforts behind him, Brooks could not have developed the command and attention he did.

Brooks's concern with the problems confronting the artistic personality was not merely academic: it was a deeply felt private affair. Before he could properly analyze the universal questions, he had first of all to achieve, like any artist, some kind of esthetic or psychic distance from himself. This detachment was attained in large measure through the dialogues he wrote, until what was personal experience became the national experience, a theme he could approach more directly. The voice he created for himself came through strong and clear in the final pages of *The Malady of the Ideal*. In Amiel, the concluding study of the book, he had found an objective correlative for his private sensibility. His portrait of Amiel, as Brooks sketched it, provided the silhouette against which he subsequently cast his outlines of other artistic personalities.

In addition, the lesson he read from Amiel's thwarted career led him to state for himself the function of criticism. In confronting books and men, he said, the critic should ask of them: "How far do they enlarge our conception of human destiny, how far do they increase the human scale, add to the number of ways in which personality can achieve itself?" For him, criticism and history, like tragedy, had each its catharsis: "The one as regards individuals, the other as regards race, the purgation of human life from its alloys, its obstructions." Moreover, the record of Amiel's incomplete personality had value for Brooks, and he asserted its value for others: "Life, we feel, ought to be of such a character that every personality can be free to realize itself. And it is only by the study of personality that we can understand the obstructions that exist in the world and the methods of removing them."[2]

Although the emphasis in this statement is a psychological one, it is essentially an introspective one, even though Brooks maintained some distance from himself by directing the remark at Amiel. Derived from his own idealistic self and from an eclectic reading among kindred minds, the commitment Brooks made is almost like that of the psychoanalyst. The critic becomes a kind of therapist; he aims at the removal of obstructions to fulfillment—through an understanding of what they are. The psychological emphasis is worth noting, however, because Brooks has sometimes been singled out, especially for *The Ordeal of Mark Twain*, as one of the first American critics to make use of psychoanalytic ideas. But the evidence of this early commitment to the study of personality suggests *not* that he was an early student of Freud, as has sometimes been inferred.[3] Instead, it reveals an extension into the twentieth century of the concern of many nineteenth-century writers with the subjective processes of art and creation.

What is new, perhaps, and what made the writings of Freud useful to Brooks and others of his generation when they became available, was Brooks's emphasis upon the need to *remove* the obstructions that stood in the artist's way. It is also noteworthy that before Freud's work became popular and added to the hue and cry against Puritanism as a "repressive" force in American life, Brooks had already identified the Puritan as an obstruction. In *The Malady of the Ideal* he emphatically "resented" the creed of Calvinism (readily equated with Puritanism and with Protestantism generally) that had prevented Amiel from becoming a poet.

I *John Addington Symonds, Victim of Puritanism*

John Addington Symonds: A Biographical Study is really another examination of a victim of the malady of the ideal and, except for the change in style and tone, might have been included in the earlier book. The difference in tone, however, is an important one. The lyrical quality of the earlier essays is absent, and the theme of a personal quest has become converted into a thesis. The pronouncements are made definitively, with sureness and conviction. The voice of the critic judges the personality of Symonds, points warningly to the obstructions, and pronounces a verdict upon them.

The structure and plan of the book are the same Brooks was to follow with more skill in the later study of Mark Twain. Judgment is made at the outset: Symonds was a tragic victim. There follows an exploration of "suggestive" biographical facts gleaned from letters, diaries, and anecdotes—each arranged to reveal the conflict between inner and outer nature. Reliance upon extra-literary evidence became, in fact, a distinguishing trait of Brooks's criticism.

The objective of the study of Symonds became, in addition, that of much of his subsequent criticism: to unravel the "tragedy underneath" which was, he said, "the modern story." Brooks thereafter addressed always the present, the modern scene. The series of portraits of the artist as victim provided a composite type in which many a contemporary of Brooks professed to see himself. The pattern of obstructions which Brooks sketched in Symonds' life story, a pattern similar to Amiel's, was repeated again and again until it became a formula. American writers who came of age just before World War I were often in remarkable agreement when they recalled how their own ardent selves had been buffeted between their desire to create and the demands of a heavily moralistic environment—as in the case of Randolph Bourne's *History of a Literary Radical* and Floyd Dell's *Homecoming*. Brooks's *John Addington Symonds* has value today less for what it says about Symonds than as a portrait in which American writers of a pre-war generation saw themselves.

A virtual feud between the older and younger generations in America was brewing during the years when the voice of Brooks the critic was emerging, and *John Addington Symonds* and his next work, *The World of H. G. Wells*, are best understood as contributions to this debate. The antagonists in the story of Symonds were the elder Symonds and Benjamin Jowett, the translator of Plato and young Symonds' tutor. In both men Brooks saw mirrored the puritanic features of "the older generation." Jowett, for instance, he saw as "a great doctor of the mundane, equipped with tonics and lotions for all the miasmas of youth. . . . He was one of those worldly men who seem to be justified by their inexorable sense of duty. . . . He believed so strongly in duty, in work, in government, in rank, system, form, the *fait accompli*, because he did not believe at all in life, in human nature, in the soul."[4]

Symonds himself, on the other hand, reflected the emotional and ideological affinities of Brooks's generation. Like Symonds, Amiel, and the two young speakers in *The Wine of the Puritans*, the members of this younger generation often expressed the feeling that they should have been living in another world and not, as they found to their distaste, "among the kind of men who build empires," who looked upon any "lack of system" as a weakness, who could not appreciate an Emerson for whom "the lack of system . . . is the essential condition of all illuminated thought." Like Symonds, this pre-war generation found in Whitman a powerful restorative influence. Like Symonds, they too accepted "that modern view" of science, "not as a destroyer, but as a builder." For that reason, too, they had made of H. G. Wells their prophet, and the Wellsian world which Brooks described for them was actually their world, the one they wanted to live in because, as Brooks put it, it rested on a "faith in human nature" and not on denial.

II   *H. G. Wells: A Model for Americans*

There came a time—almost within months, in fact, of the publication of Brooks's study—when H. G. Wells, along with other
idols like John Dewey, tumbled from the high pedestal on which
the younger generation had set him. One can see the ironic reversal in the reception given the publication, in 1916, of Wells's
Mr. Britling Sees It Through. Stuart Sherman, who had seized
the opportunity in his review of Brooks's *World of H. G. Wells*
to mock with stinging irony both Wells and his young American
idolators, hailed the *Britling* book as a sign of Wells's conversion
and as a vindication of humanist principles. Randolph Bourne,
on the other hand, spoke of the disillusionment of younger critics
when he pronounced Wells's "discovery" of a finite God a failure
to "see it through," and sadly declared that Wells was no longer
a reliable, intelligent force. But Brooks's tribute to the Wellsian
vision of a socialist world was written and published before the
war provoked a clash of loyalties. It is, therefore, especially revealing of the hopeful mood during that last age of innocence
in America.

Throughout *The World of H. G. Wells,* Brooks placed special
emphasis upon Wells's socialism and the "connection" between
it and America. Socialism in general, he said, had already shown
that society was "a colossal machine" in which all men were
members. Wells had taken socialism one step further by showing that society was a world of intelligence "already exuberant
with instinct." Wells had done for the "social organism," said
Brooks in a significant metaphorical shift, what Wordsworth had
done for nature: he had endowed it with "a personality," making
it "a matter for art and a basis for religious emotion." The special
connection between Wells and America, according to Brooks,
lay in the way Wells's career demonstrated the need to bring
about a coherent relationship between the world of ideas and
that of experience before society's personality could be fully
realized.

Wells had commenced his career as an intellectual who saw
life in the light of ideas rather than of experience. But he had
reached a point in his career when ideas had lost their substance
for him, and Brooks quoted approvingly Wells's admonition to
"reject all such ideas as Right, Liberty, Happiness, Duty, and
Beauty and hold fast to the assertion of the fundamental nature

of life as a tissue and succession of births"—which anticipates Hemingway's more famous declaration in *A Farewell to Arms* that such abstract words were obscene alongside the concrete names that signified experience. Brooks saw Wells's career as moving toward the fathoming of the nature of human experience, leaving behind most orthodox notions of socialism, abandoning economics in favor of psychology, and developing a universe where things were "infinitely plastic." Wells had learned, said Brooks, that life could not be determined by ideas alone. Brooks judged that in at least two books, *Tono-Bungay* and *The New Machiavelli,* Wells had achieved a proper balance, making ideas and experience meet "in a certain invisible point. . . . The greatest possible faith in ideas was united with the greatest possible grasp of everything that impedes them." Wells had demonstrated that "theory divorced from practice is a mode of charlatanism."

It was in America, especially, of all the countries of Western civilization, that the chasm between the worlds of ideas and of experience was most evident. Somewhat dogmatically Brooks commented:

> For this there is only one salvation. If civilization has lost the faculty of commanding itself and pulling itself together in its individual aspect, it must pull itself together collectively. That essentially is the fighting chance of intellectualism. . . . From this follows the oft-repeated phrase of Wells that the chief want of the American people is a "sense of the state." For the peril and hope of American life (granting that, as things are, society must be brought into some kind of coherence before morality, art and religion can once more attain any real meaning) lies in the fact that while at present Americans are aware of themselves only as isolated individuals they are unconsciously engaged in works of an almost appalling significance for the future of society.

These "works," "rudiments of the Socialist State, falsely based . . . but always tending to subvert this false basis," were such as the Trusts, the Rockefeller Institute, the Carnegie and Russell Sage foundations, the endowed universities and bureaus of research, and "the type of men they breed." The question was whether the financial mind would learn to yield to the greater mind of "the race."[5]

This criticism was neither literary nor social. The point of view was aimed not solely at Wells as an artist, nor at Wells as a social philosopher, but at the connection between the literary mind and the mind involved in the social world. Wells's career suggested to Brooks that the two need not fly apart in mutual repugnance and to a mutually sterile end. Wells had come to terms with tradition; and yet he had preserved his artist's soul, his individual vision, and had done so in fact largely by his uses of tradition: by seeing society as an integrated personality. He conceived of society as being, like a work of art, governed by organic principles. For Brooks, Wells provided a model for the artist America needed: one who would find and make use of an American tradition that bridged the worlds of ideas and of experience.

III *Highbrow and Lowbrow*

The final chapter of the book on Wells, emphasizing the Englishman's Americanism, probably provided the momentum which led Brooks to write *America's Coming-of-Age*. He had ended *The World of H. G. Wells* with an observation about the split in America between ideas and experience, and he opened his next book with an epigraph that stated his thesis about America: "The middle of humanity thou never knewest, but the extremity of both ends." This he applied, patly and succinctly, to his judgment about the American past, and phrased it within a paragraph:

> So it is that from the beginning we find two main currents in the American mind running side by side but rarely mingling—a current of overtones and a current of undertones—and both equally unsocial: on the one hand, the transcendental current, originating in the piety of the Puritans, becoming a philosophy in Jonathan Edwards, passing through Emerson, producing the fastidious refinement and aloofness of the chief American writers, and resulting in the final unreality of most contemporary culture; and on the other hand the current of catchpenny opportunism, originating in the practical shifts of Puritan life, becoming a philosophy in Franklin, passing through the American humorists, and resulting in the atmosphere of our contemporary business life.[6]

These two attitudes of mind had been phrased in the American vernacular as "Highbrow" and "Lowbrow," both derogatory terms. "The 'Highbrow' is the superior person whose virtue is admitted but felt to be an inept unpalatable virtue; while the 'Lowbrow' is a good fellow one readily takes to, but with a certain scorn for him and all his works." They were both undesirable, as personal types and what they stood for, "but they divide American life between them" (4).

The judgment that American life lay divided by two extremes, "Highbrow" and "Lowbrow," with an undefined chasm between, was hardly original with Brooks. The vastness, multiplicity, and heterogeneity of America has long confounded historians and other students of national character in search of some one explanatory key. What they have often come up with has been two sets of keys—one for a tradition of American idealism; one for American materialism. Frequently deplored, sometimes cited as a source of strength, the paradox is not easily resolved.

In 1876, William Graham Sumner, in a centennial review of American politics, had declared in language very much like Brooks's that a breach had opened following the feud between the leaders of the Federalist party and John Adams, one that had widened and had been as harmful to culture as to politics: "On the one side it has been left to anti-culture to control all which is indigenous and 'American'; and on the other hand American culture has been like a plant in a thin soil, given over to sickly dilettantism and the slavish imitation of foreign models, ill understood, copied for matters of form, and, as often as not, imitated for their worst defects."[7]

Walt Whitman, in *Democratic Vistas* (the "Bible of American writers," Brooks later called it) had pointed to the same separation of those "genteel little creatures" whose "perpetual, pistareen, pastepot work" was taken for American art, from the "practical life" which had as yet no place in a program of culture. Identity, national identity—"Personalism" was his word for it—was what Whitman sought. Henry Adams, perplexed by the same phenomenon and capable of a long historical view, found suggestive explanations in the symbolism of the Virgin of the thirteenth century and in the Dynamo of the twentieth. When *The Education of Henry Adams* was finally given to the public in 1918, Brooks and the writers he had spoken for found that it confirmed their own sense of America's dilemma. Closer still to Brooks's statement in time and spirit was George Santayana's essay, "The Genteel Tradition in American Philosophy," delivered first as a lecture in the summer of 1911 and printed in *Winds of Doc-*

trine (1913)—a book which entered the lists on the side of the younger generation. In his essay, the spirit of "aggressive enterprise" matched Brooks's Lowbrow and "the genteel tradition" his Highbrow; moreover, Santayana found the common origin, as Brooks had, in an earlier Calvinism.

If not original in his observation of a divided American mind, Brooks nevertheless phrased it at the right historical moment and in words that proved highly suggestive. He gave renewed and vigorous currency to a thesis about America that soon became commonplace and that still carries some conviction. American scholars, critics, and historians continue to echo him and to explore the paradox of an America of high ideals and catchpenny opportunism.[8]

One concludes that the source of Brooks's original power lay in his helping to resurrect an image of the Puritan as the chief obstruction to the fulfillment of a national personality. At a time when moralism was being questioned on all sides as it conflicted with pressing need for practical actions, Brooks brought the blurred sentiments of uncertainty into focus upon a fabulous character, the Puritan in the American past and present. He thus provoked Americans into re-examining the sources of their ideals and their behavior as found in the Puritan image. *America's Coming-of-Age*—or as Brooks once intended to call it, *A Fable for Yankees*—would not have made itself felt as it did, however, had there not been some strong half-truths lurking behind the image and speaking the poetic truth that national fables often contain.

It is not easy to account for the apparent overnight change from national reverence and pious respect for the heritage of the Puritan to outright mockery and scorn of it. One can note the expression of national pride on the very eve of this change, in 1908, in a respectable magazine like the *Dial,* which assured its readers that American culture rested firmly on "the granite of puritan character," and that "fine flowers of ethical order and patriotism," like Bryant, Longfellow and Whittier, Hawthorne, Lowell, and Emerson, had grown from the soil adhering to that stone. And then, one may get some measure of the change that occurred in noting the irony that the same magazine, under new management, awarded Van Wyck Brooks a prize in 1924 for a career in criticism which up to that point was distinguished largely by his role in converting those "fine flowers" into "noxious weeds" and by his having called the Puritan soil a tainted one.

One can chart the rise of anti-Puritanism until it became a serious attitude among young writers and critics between these years. Thereafter, during the war, it grew in intensity, and then was flattened out into triteness under the rhetorical barrage of Mencken and his followers in the 1920's. The critical documents may be singled out: all of Brooks's early work; Santayana's essays; Randolph Bourne's *Seven Arts* essays, especially "The Puritan's Will-to-Power" (April, 1917); Mencken's *A Book of Prefaces* with its guiding essay, "Puritanism as a Literary Force" (1917); and Waldo Frank's *Our America* (1919). But the way Puritanism became a dominant theme in American fiction, drama, and poetry was not (and has not been) fully explored. Still, where this theme appeared it was largely an extension of the metaphorical onslaught launched by these critics against the Puritan in American life. However it is explained—or wherever it provided, in Brooks's phrase, "the resisting background" against which an analysis of some area in American life was cast—Brooks's role in releasing and exploiting the metaphor of Puritanism remains a primary one.

In a wider and longer historical perspective, the anti-Puritan quarrel might be explained as a mere symptom of deeper forces at work, reflecting the clash between the traditional and more nearly absolute values of an older, agrarian, predominantly Anglo-Saxon order and the newer values of an emerging industrial and urban society of new immigrant origin. But whatever the way of accounting for the anti-Puritanism of those years just before and after World War I, the fact of the omnipresence of the Puritan in the American imagination must be recognized. The essential question is not so much what the Puritan symbolized, but how and for what reason the symbol was used.

Having arrived at a point of view that saw the work of art in terms of personality, as fulfillment, and the task of the critic to remove the obstructions to that end, Brooks commenced in earnest the ambitious task of creating the kind of conditions in America that would permit personalities to complete themselves. Viewing art metaphorically as personality, he saw obstructions to art in the same kinds of metaphor—and chief among these was the personality of the Puritan.

America's Coming-of-Age is what Brooks first entitled it: a fable. ("The America Myth" had been still another proposed title.) It tells of the divided personality of America—as it is and as it was, "once upon a time." The opening words were actually "At the time when . . . ." The moral of his tale, as every good fable has its moral, is that this is not as it will be, for "after all humanity is older than Puritanism" (the final words in the book).

The style was liberally marked by the rhetorical flourishes of the fabulist at work—"as it were," "so to speak," "so to say"—and these betray the metaphorical method of his argument. The "preciselys" thundering on every other page force the analogies where no precision is possible. The "without doubts," the "meanings" always so "full of," provide that air of profound truth every good fable seems to exhale. The damning rhetorical questions channel the answers to point a moral: "What side of American life is not touched by this antithesis [of Highbrow and Lowbrow]? What explanation of American life is more central or more illuminating? In everything one finds this frank acceptance of twin values which are not expected to have anything in common: on the one hand a quite unclouded, quite unhypocritical assumption of transcendent theory ('high ideals'); on the other a simultaneous acceptance of catchpenny realities" (3).

Finally, however, the skill with which Brooks filled out his portrait of divided America in a series of deft references to American personalities of the past and present gave his fable its semblance of truth. His catchwords did catch at the bottom of things where, as he said, the question was really "a personal one" —one to be seen, that is, in terms of actual personalities. From his opening reference to William Jennings Bryan, through his projection of Jonathan Edwards as archetypal Highbrow and Ben Franklin as Lowbrow, through his ironically cast portraits of "Our Poets," to a final memorable image of America as a vast Sargasso Sea, Brooks gave concrete expression to his revulsion before the "stench of atrophied personality" that was America. Behind each reference hovered the blighting presence of the Puritan.

It is a little surprising that the fable in *America's Coming-of-Age* has so often been overlooked, for Brooks was quite candid in revealing his hand. As he prepared to examine "Our Poets," he bluntly announced, "It is a principle that shines impartially on the just and the unjust that once you have a point of view all history will back you up"—a rather bald confession of the relativity of historical evidence. He was even more candid as he approached his conclusion: "Issues which really make the life of a society do not spring spontaneously out of the mass. They exist in it—a thousand potential currents and cross-currents; but they have to be discovered like principles of science, they have almost to be created like works of art" (85).

It would, in fact, be hard to say whether the issue of Puritanism as it was raised by Brooks had been discovered in the cross-currents of American life, or created—given a form and coherence that was the truth of appearance rather than of reality. That it was more nearly a creation is suggested not only by Brooks's hints in the pages of *America's Coming-of-Age* itself, but also by his subsequent tendency to dismiss as a straw man the Puritan he and his contemporaries had attacked in the pre-war years.

To describe *America's Coming-of-Age* as a fable, and the central issue it raised as an artificially created one, is not, however, to disparage its criticism as invalid; on the contrary, it is simply to suggest why it was so effective, why it was capable of stirring a whole generation of young American writers into rebellion. The image of the Puritan as the obstructing force yielded to a series of others—pioneers, professors, George Babbitts. Each was a Puritan in new dress. But each was a personal metaphor which every member of the younger generation could, and did, fill out with the concrete images of actual people. What Brooks provided writers was the habit of making a personal identification with America.

The very title of the book, *America's Coming-of-Age*, is of course drawn from the language applied to the growth of personality. Brooks's cocky announcement that America was on the verge of a burst of creativity touched the ambitions of young men who were feeling their own growth. Their first response was that of the rebel, and with joy in their hearts (because they knew beforehand that success was theirs) they turned upon the past and upon their elders. *America's Coming-of-Age* gave them a theory of the American past to account for their abomination of both the crude Philistinism and the vapid idealism of the present; it gave them also a brilliant justification of their irreverence toward the canonized figures of "Our Poets"; but it also reassured them that they had a positive cause and an exciting precedent in Walt Whitman.

Each of the literary figures Brooks examined in "Our Poets" has been restudied and reassessed many times since 1915, but, on the whole, there is little need to revise the judgments Brooks made of them then. True, he made no "rounded estimates" and was more concerned with making each poet fill out his thesis in order to demonstrate how American literary history would back up his point of view. Yet, granting his naturalistic criterion—the extent to which the writing of "Our Poets" was connected to the American actuality—little issue can be taken with his observations on Bryant, Longfellow, Irving, Cooper, Poe, and Hawthorne, and certainly not with his measurement of Lowell. Only Brooks's strictures on Emerson, especially on his style (like "a continual falsetto"), and on Transcendentalism were marked by a personal spleen—a bias to which, incidentally, he openly confessed. But even here Brooks's quarrel was not with Emerson himself (for he alone, said Brooks, of all American writers had given "some kind of basis to American idealism") so much as with Emersonianism. On this score, as a reading of the influence of the Emersonian doctrine of self-reliance upon the development and expansion of nineteenth-century America, there is little to take issue with.

Brooks's *America's Coming-of-Age,* in short, still speaks with some authority to the contemporary mind and records the brilliance of his insights when he first uttered them. For what he said was by no means so acceptable in 1915 as in the 1960's. It is a little difficult to capture from our present-day perspective the reverence and awe with which official America viewed its cultural figures in the 1910's. It helps if, in some dusty attic, one has run across the kind of paneled picture frame which used to enshrine them, and then has read Brooks's description: "What emotions pass through an hereditary American when he calls to mind the worthies who figured in that ubiquitous group of 'Our Poets' which occupied once so prominent a place in so many domestic interiors! Our Poets were commonly six in number, kindly, grey-bearded, or otherwise grizzled old men. One recalls a prevailing six, with variations. Sometimes a venerable historian was included, a novelist or so, and even Bayard Taylor" (21).

"Even Bayard Taylor" helps the contemporary reader to realize what emotions must have run through Brooks's first readers who knew that panel at closer hand. It was a good stroke of irony, better appreciated then than now, when for the most part a reference to Bayard Taylor has lost its meaning. This kind of irony, playing throughout his examination of "Our Poets," made convincing to his generation Brooks's summary disposal of them:

> Taken as a whole the most characteristic fact about them is a certain delicacy which arrives in literature almost in the degree to which it stands remote from life, achieves its own salvation (after the Puritan fashion) by avoiding contact with actuality. . . . This is the whole story of American literature: in a more than usually difficult and sordid world, it has applied its principal energies to being uncontaminated itself. It has held aloof, as a consciously better part, like all American idealism. The talent is there, high and dry; and if it is not always too high, it is very often a great deal too dry (57-58).

It was a tonic declaration. Healthy too was the rescue role Brooks performed for his generation in saving Whitman from the Whitmanians. The positive side of his thesis, and that which made *America's Coming-of-Age* a manifesto, lay in its singling out Whitman as the precursor of a "middle tradition," one effectively combining theory and action, one in whom "the hitherto incompatible extremes of the American temperament were fused." (Brooks had already said of Emerson that "the upper and lower levels of the American mind are fused in him," perfectly combining the temperaments of Jonathan Edwards and Benjamin Franklin—a contradiction Brooks expunged from the revised edition. It was a slip that anticipated Brooks's rediscovery of Emerson, however, and suggests only that it was more difficult to isolate Emerson from the Emersonians than Whitman from the Whitmanians.)

Whitman's significance for America, for Brooks and his generation, lay in his providing "the sense of something organic in American life." He had challenged—as Brooks was urging his fellows to do—"the abnormal dignity of American letters." He provided a *"focal centre,"* by which, said Brooks, he did not mean a sense of national or imperial destiny, but "that national 'point of rest,' to adopt a phrase in which Coleridge indicated that upon which the harmony of a work of art is founded and to which everything in the composition is more or less unconsciously referred"—an analogy which reveals again Brooks's propensity for viewing art, society, and personality as integrated wholes, each concentric upon the other, or, in Emersonian fashion, as correspondences of each other.

Whitman, however, although he had laid a cornerstone of a national ideal, provided only a collection of raw materials—materials properly conducive to the right emotional attitude—but he was without "the ideas that are to inform it." In the America of his time, said Brooks, Whitman, to affirm sufficiently, had had to affirm everything. Acting as spokesman for his own generation, Brooks said, "We are in a different position, and we have different responsibilities. . . . Above all, we have no excuse not to see that affirmation, in the most real sense, proceeds to a certain extent through rejection, by merely dropping off most of the old clothes that Whitman found quite good enough" (67).

This notion of "affirmation through rejection" became a central attitude among American writers that was acted upon in varying degrees up to the extreme gesture of expatriatism. In more subtle ways it led to the satiric mode and tones of irony of much writing in the 1920's. Besides defining the sources of their complaints, *America's Coming-of-Age* provided young American writers with a rationale for their style—both in behavior and in writing. They became self-conscious rebels, self-styled literary radicals, who were dedicated to destroy in order to build.

Others besides Brooks had contributed to the growth of "Young America's" self-consciousness—Randolph Bourne, for instance, in a series of *Atlantic Monthly* essays (collected in *Youth and Life*, 1913) on characteristic themes like "The Dodging of Pressures," "The Experimental Life," "The Life of Irony," and "For Radicals." And Walter Lippmann, whose *Drift and Mastery* (1914) preceded *America's Coming-of-Age* by only a few months, had spoken in the same way to his contemporaries: "So far as we are concerned, then, the case is made out against absolutism, commercial oligarchy, and unquestioned creeds. *The rebel program is stated* [Lippmann's emphasis]. Scientific invention and blind social currents have made the old authority impossible in fact, the artillery fire of the iconoclasts has shattered its prestige. We inherit a rebel tradition." But *America's Coming-of-Age* was the more stirring fable, and, appearing at a moment when some members of the older generation flattered the young with stern rebukes, it sent a shock of recognition through "Young America."

CHAPTER 4

The Literary Leader

THE FORCES of literary criticism prevailing in the decade when Brooks established himself as a leader of the younger generation are not easy to sift, separate, and define. In *America's Coming-of-Age* Brooks himself alluded to only two critical camps —the "old-fashioned" nationalistic school that in effect surrendered the right to criticize in favor of national pride, and the "contemporary camp" whose method, Brooks said, was one of constant "depreciative comparison with better folk than our own." Professor Barrett Wendell, who was at Harvard when Brooks was a student, might reasonably have been representative of the first camp, and Professor Irving Babbitt of the second. It became common practice on the part of younger critics, however, to link the two groups under the common derisive epithet, "the professors."

This classification was not altogether fair to academic critics, for professors then as now resisted identification with groups. But the professors were in charge, and academicians were, by and large, the molders of American literary opinion. Santayana was not far from the truth in singling out the American university as the last stronghold of the genteel tradition, however premature he was in announcing its passing. The precedent for the sniping against professors and pedants which Mencken made into a popular pastime appears throughout *America's Coming-of-Age*. As the appointed conservators of the past, professors were natural targets for the rebellious young men. What most of the academic critics did share was, at worst, a common abhorrence of, and, at best, a common indifference toward most contemporary literature. They presented a spectacle that documented only too well Brooks's charge that in America art was kept chastely remote from life.

One small group of "professors" soon emerged, however, and

these contributed a coherent body of critical work with a recognizable identity: humanism, or rather, the *new* humanism. Irving Babbitt, Brooks's teacher, was its chief expounder, Paul Elmer More its most eloquent practitioner, and Stuart Sherman, their younger disciple, its most passionate and belligerent defender. They were few, but the critical movement they began was highly influential.

The work of these three men had all the appearance of an intimate collaboration—a "conspiracy" to the younger critics who challenged them. Babbitt's studies, marred by a good deal of word-mongering, presented a sustained indictment of every aspect of modern art; he judged it decadent and diseased, the result of influences at work since the advent of Rousseau and of the romantic heresies he had released. Romanticism, departing from the philosophical dualism of the ancients, had, according to Babbitt, caused standards to disintegrate, had blurred the necessary distinctions among the genres of art, and had given rise to sentimental humanitarianism, naturalism, estheticism, and impressionism. The only corrective was for men to exercise again the humanist principle of restraint—of an inner check—in order to preserve separately the law for man and the law for thing.

Paul Elmer More, who from 1901-1914 served, first, as editor of the *Independent,* the literary review of the New York *Evening Post,* and then the *Nation,* was in a strategic position to advance the humanist creed. He was a more graceful writer than Babbitt; and, because he dealt more often with particulars, he more readily drew the fire of young writers like Van Wyck Brooks. His eighth volume of *Shelburne Essays, The Drift of Romanticism* (1913), showed him to be in open league with Babbitt. This was the same year Brooks had published *The Malady of the Ideal,* his poetic tribute to the anguished romantic soul, and it was part of the "drift" More tried to stem. Curiously, both books spoke of romanticism as a sickness; one considered it an affliction of the individual artist; the other, of the whole modern era. They differed, however, in their diagnosis of what was symptom and what was cause. For Brooks, the malady came from the individual artist's failure to achieve "one-ness," from his inability to reconcile the claims of tradition with those of his own talent or his own vision of the ideal. For More, it was the attempt itself to throw over tradition in favor of the anarchic self that encouraged the drift toward disintegration and disease.

Stuart Sherman made his start as a critic in his writing for the New York *Evening Post,* for which he served a brief year in 1908 as editor, and then for the *Nation.* He was a professor first of all, but he made his mark in New York literary journalism. Though he might have qualified as a member of the younger generation, he auditioned instead for the role of teacher and counselor to his contemporaries. Where his masters Babbitt and More were always profound and highly serious, Sherman matched the tones of irony of the rebellious critics with a strident mockery of his own. In book reviews and essays he lashed out at all the foes of humanism, noting the baleful effect upon the egotism of "Young America" of the winds of doctrine coming from William James, Bernard Shaw, H. G. Wells, and other favorites of young men. His essay review of Brooks's *The World of H. G. Wells* was a full-scale lecture aimed at correcting the younger generation's ignorance of the past, and at exposing the sentimental nonsense in the thinking of their prophet, Wells, by a contrast with the thinking of Matthew Arnold—with whom Brooks had dared make a "grotesque" comparison. Reviewing *America's Coming-of-Age,* Sherman uttered a mild guffaw at Brooks's socialism; he had closed the book, he said, with the sound in his ears of "an uproar in the street caused by a crowd of cowboys and a crowd of college professors."[1]

This figure was an apt one—more so than even Sherman guessed—and a prophecy of the uproar that shortly followed. Sherman's sharp jibes at the younger critics helped, in fact, to drive them into a loose federation that appeared to be a unified movement. The writers who gathered around Max Eastman and Floyd Dell on the *Masses,* H. L. Mencken and George Jean Nathan on the *Smart Set,* Herbert Croly, Walter Lippmann, and Francis Hackett on the *New Republic,* and James Oppenheim, Waldo Frank, Randolph Bourne, and Brooks on the *Seven Arts* had much in common; and their writings frequently appeared in one another's magazines. Most of all, they had youth, and they rendered that fact into a principle of criticism.

These young critics commonly assumed that the first task of criticism in America and in their time was to clear the ground of everything that kept art and life from growing in some harmonious relationship to each other. As critics, therefore, they were more often engaged in attacks on the literature of the past than in defense or explication of the new writing. Their common instrument, irony, ranged from the horselaughs and shotgun blasts that came from the *Smart Set* writers to the more urbane wit of Brooks and to the gentler yet stinging criticism in the *New Republic* of Santayana. They commonly attacked standards, traditions, and morality—as principles for judging literature. They herded together and branded all professors as Puritans, purists, pedants, and Philistines.

Later, after the war, this unity among the younger critics broke down to form a host of critical groups—Marxist, Freudian, nationalist and historical, and Mencken's followers who maintained an impressionistic tradition resting on naturalistic premises. Brooks, who contributed to each of these, never committed himself wholly to any one camp; he thus retained, in the body of his critical writings thereafter, something of the unified movement that had prevailed before 1920.

One other critical point of view, however, had been slowly formulating in the prewar years. Primarily esthetic and formalist, it had been a quiet accompaniment to the poetic renaissance. It assumed the autonomy of works of art and dedicated itself to a close reading of the literary text itself, to the primacy of the word, and to analysis of associations not only within the work of art but between the reader and the image or literary form confronting him. The leadership which gave this point of view direction and inspiration came from the poetry and criticism first of Ezra Pound and then, after the appearance of *The Waste Land* (1922), more and more from the work of T. S. Eliot. To be sure, there were others who practiced, defended, and explicated the formalist approach to the critique of literature, but when a definable critical movement appeared much later calling itself "The New Criticism," it was apparent that Eliot had been the chief guide and exemplar of "the New Critics." Until then, the critics who had shared some of its assumptions, or had at least declared their sympathy with them, were simply called "esthetes."

Brooks very early set himself against the esthetic critic and his formalist point of view. His long-standing opposition to Eliot and the new criticism, amounting at times almost to a feud, had early beginnings. His suspicion of rhetoric, for instance, and his identification of the malady of the ideal with an artist's over-concern for technique were anticipatory signs. But only when theoretician Joel E. Spingarn appeared, arguing strongly if abstractly for an esthetic creed in America free of all the usual academic approaches to literature, did Brooks openly enter himself against the esthete.

Spingarn, a professor of comparative literature at Columbia University, was a rebel among the professors. He had made the study of literary criticism his special preserve and had promoted the critical approach of his friend and idol, the Italian philosopher and critic, Benedetto Croce. In 1910, Spingarn, contributing to a Columbia series of lectures on literature, delivered one on literary criticism, an essay he later called "The New Criticism," in which he calmly declared obsolete every criterion for judging literature used by his colleagues.

When the lectures were collected and published in *Columbia University Lectures on Literature* (1911), the agreement among other professors was remarkable. One reviewer for the *Nation* noted with approval the "lack of antagonism." But he had overlooked Spingarn's concluding essay which not only dismissed the others as obsolete but challenged the whole framework of the series with its neat division of literature into periods, genres, movements, influences, and origins. Art was "organic expression," said Spingarn, and each work of art was governed by its own law. It was senseless, therefore, to demand or expect it to conform to any other rule. So away with all the old formulas and standards. Most of all, said Spingarn, "we have done with all moral judgment of literature." To him, "no critic of authority now tests literature by the standards of ethics."

This was heady stuff, polemical, intended to stir debate. It did, but only in academic circles, where Spingarn's revolt was analyzed as springing from a discontent with the scholar's arduous tasks; or in conservative journals like the *Dial,* which asserted anew that the business of criticism was "to account for literature," "to justify it" and "to admit the validity of the judgments upon which the moralists have been united."[2] Even Randolph Bourne, not yet arrived at his own radical position, declared that Spingarn, in ruling out all that savored of the ethical, was inviting "the suicide of criticism"; and he referred his fellow students at Columbia to "the sane and healthy message" of Irving Babbitt. Babbitt himself ignored the disciple for the master and disdainfully lumped Signor Croce with other anti-intellectuals who perpetuated romantic heresies.

Not until Spingarn republished this essay, along with others, in his *Creative Criticism: Essays on the Unity of Genius and Taste* (1917) did he attract some support from other critics who were revolting against the professors. Mencken singled him out as one of the few "campus critics" worth listening to, and the *Seven Arts* gave Spingarn space to expound his views. But the rebellion of the young men was their own by then, and they would not readily yield it to follow a professor, however compatible they might find some of his views. Their acknowledged leader, Van Wyck Brooks, told them why they should be wary of professors when he answered Spingarn and other academic critics in the magazine the young writers had created for their rebellion.

The *Seven Arts* was directly inspired by Van Wyck Brooks; and James Oppenheim, its founding editor along with Waldo Frank, wrote later of how their discovery of a new book, *America's Coming-of-Age,* had provoked the plan for *"the* magazine" that would mobilize the native talent Brooks called for. Paul Rosenfeld, who shortly joined Oppenheim and Frank, also recalled their common awareness "of the unity of the phenomena of the pioneersman and of the American art of the past and transcendentalism and pragmatism," and how Brooks's book had persuaded them they were correct in perceiving that unity. And Frank, writing to invite Brooks to join them in their venture, called *America's Coming-of-Age* the "prologemena [*sic*] to our Future Seven Arts Magazine."[3]

When the first number appeared in November, 1916, the announcement of its purpose revealed that it had enlisted in the service of Van Wyck Brooks's critical creed. It was "to become a channel for the flow of . . . new tendencies: an expression of American life. . . . not a magazine for artists but an expression of artists for the community." Its succeeding numbers amply lived up to this intention, but its writing was largely directed *at* the American community in a steadily mounting criticism of its failure to sustain the life of art. Brooks's contributions, appearing in seven of the magazine's twelve numbers, set the tone of the attack and also singled out the chief areas of culpability.

I *Youth and Tradition*

Following the demise of the magazine, Brooks collected these essays under the title *Letters and Leadership* (1918). Like *Amer-*

ica's Coming-of-Age—to which it is appended in later editions of that book—it was not literary criticism. However, it had much to say about "letters" and the state of "an organized higher life," that was defined as "a literature fully aware of the difficulties of the American situation and able, in some sense, to meet them." Chiefly, the book is about "the difficulties of the American situation." Brooks justified it as criticism by his reliance on Matthew Arnold's famous dictum that the business of criticism was "to make an intellectual situation of which the creative power can profitably avail itself."

Not as a contribution to literary criticism, but as a species of criticism peculiarly American, *Letters and Leadership* is in the tradition of Emerson's *American Scholar* and Walt Whitman's *Democratic Vistas* (which Brooks quoted at length). Brooks, in a kind of stock-taking of the national resources of spirit and mind, is at once denunciatory and exhortative as he points to "the conditions that hamper [America's] creative life" in order to prepare the way for a "synthesis of the creative energies of the younger generation."

In the context of the historical episode which the *Seven Arts* contains—those months of sharpening national debate about and then final involvement in World War I—Brooks's articles played a lively, meaningful role. The war in Europe, in 1916 a war without a future, seemed to many Americans to have imperiled civilization itself and to have placed a special cultural responsibility upon them. The *Seven Arts,* which consciously assumed this responsibility, belligerently announced that a new day had come, that Americans could no longer indulge in the questionable luxury of cultural provincialism, and that the acquisitive impulse heretofore characteristic of American behavior would have to yield to the creative impulse. Henceforth art and artists would provide the leadership that would create a genuine civilization, a corporate community. Brooks's articles gave shape to each of these themes and provided the choric commentary on the dramatic evidence in each of the *Seven Arts* issues that a generation of American writers *was* prepared to accept the responsibility and the leadership.

When the first issue appeared in November, 1916, it featured a challenge from France—from Romain Rolland—for American writers to seize the opportunity the war in Europe had presented them. "You have been born of a soil that is neither encumbered nor shut in by past spiritual edifices," he wrote. Speaking from the misery of his own people, he explained that "There is in you no weariness of the yesterdays; no clutterings of the past." Behind American writers stood the inspiration alone of "your Homer: Walt Whitman." American writers must profit by this situation: "Be free! Do not become slaves to foreign models. Your approach to it must be the understanding of yourselves."

How much the magazine responded to this challenge is evident in the way its editors and contributors matched Rolland's stirring call to duty with their own spirit of manifesto; it shows in the self-conscious pride the magazine had for the diverse national origins of its writers and in the frequent invocations to the spirit of Walt Whitman. But, most of all, the response is evident in the self-conscious probing of the national soul that was characteristic of nearly every poem, story, and essay. In his analysis of American attitudes toward the past, trying to understand America now, in the present, in order to direct the future, Brooks led the way.

The shape Brooks gave to *Letters and Leadership* in the arrangement of his essays reveals the nature of his response to Rolland's challenge from Europe. Enveloping the *Seven Arts* essays was a preface and final chapter, "Towards the Future," written after the *Seven Arts* had folded. These two essays originally appeared as one, "War's Heritage to Youth," in the *Dial* of January 17, 1918. Chapters I and II, "Old America" ("Enterprise" in the first number of the *Seven Arts*) and "The Culture of Industrialism," examined the quality of the cultural surroundings of his own generation, specifically the individualism derived from America's past but qualified and changed by an industrial civilization. Then followed the pivotal essay, "Young America." "Our Critics" and "Our Awakeners," the two chapters following "Young America," examined the shortcomings of the intellectual leadership of the day in letters and philosophy.

But the center of hope in this patterned manifesto was youth. Brooks spoke for and to the young intellectuals of America who must accept the responsibility that Rolland said a weary, aged, and now warring Europe could no longer assume. Brooks was quite explicit when he pointed out in the last chapter, "Towards the Future," that war in Europe had "thrown us unexpectedly back upon ourselves. How many drafts we have issued in the past . . . upon European thought, unbalanced by any investment

of our own! The younger generation have come to feel this obligation acutely."

Brooks's hope rested delicately on this one point: that the
young men he knew *felt* this obligation. Their desire, their emotional commitment to a "higher organized life," was what separated them from the American past, from the traditional leaders,
even from "our awakeners, the pragmatists." This desire, he
wrote, was fed and encouraged by the example of the young
men of other nations—"the Young Italy of Mazzini's day, the
Young Ireland of ours, the rebirth of the submerged nationalities
of Eastern Europe."

The *Seven Arts* supported this awareness of an international
conspiracy of youthful desire, and published articles on "Young
Japan" and "Young Spain" (by a young John R. Dos Passos) to
supplement Brooks's "Young America." It was possible, these
examples suggested, where the desire was strong and exalted
enough to cast off "whatever incubus of crabbed age, paralysis,
tyranny, stupidity and sloth has lain most heavily upon the people's life, checking the free development of personality." The
task was possible, but in America would be difficult.

In America, tradition was too much a matter of history, not
of living actuality. By contrast—and Brooks's sense of Europe's
organic cultural experience provided the recurring comparisons
throughout every essay—Europe, though in peril at the moment,
had still managed to keep alive its ties with its own past. The
great "traditional culture," even after the rise of a culture of industrialism which was after all not peculiar to America, still
endured in Europe. Rebels against the desiccating influences of
the industrial process, like Marx and Nietzsche, William Morris
and John Stuart Mill, Ernest Renan and Auguste Rodin, had
"kept alive the tradition of a great society and great ways of
living." The democracies of Europe were consequently richer in
self-knowledge than America.

Even Germany, pre-imperialistic Germany, provided an en-
viable example in Johann Wolfgang von Goethe who had taken
the poetic approach to life, "from within outward." Using the
resources in German memory, he had brought his people from
a "pulp-like inelastic state" (like the "Sargazzo Sea" America
appeared to Brooks) to one of dynamic unity. Russia too, which
Brooks found strikingly similar in many ways to America, had
a greater richness at the core of her national life than America.

Her intellectuals lacked the social machinery to implement their visions of reform, perhaps, but they had possessed the poetic approach: "the European approach from time immemorial." Working from tradition outward, this approach had given impetus for social reform in modern England, from Carlyle's "tremendous restatement of the spiritual principle" through those of Ruskin and Morris in the economic sphere to the English liberalism of Shaw and Wells. In America it was well nigh impossible to work "from within." What passed for tradition in America was old—"old as nothing else anywhere in the world is old . . . bloodless and worn out."

Brooks's work was a strong indictment of a cultural milieu which, if it did not possess past spiritual edifices that "shut in" young America, as Rolland would have it, provided "none of the indwelling spirit of continuity" which was Europe's possession. The encircling belt of the areas Brooks scourged was thick, stretching thin the outer membrane of faith in war's heritage to youth, and making it nearly impossible for Young America, at the center, to break through and meet the responsibility of that heritage.

A sympathetic reviewer of *Letters and Leadership* noted that "on the descriptive side [Brooks's] book is eloquent and true," that, though his presentation of the physical background was symbolic, it was nevertheless *the* American scene. Typically, in depicting all that stood in the way of the hope and principles of renewal and growth, Brooks spoke through the opposing images and metaphors that added up to age, arrested youth, sterility, bloodlessness, joylessness. The paradox of American civilization, Brooks's "descriptive side" suggested, lay in its having the frame of youth stamped with the visage of old age.

He saw this contradiction suggested in the family likeness of American towns and cities, in their sharing an "alternating aspect of life and death" with intense excitement and enterprise at their centers and the tokens of burnt-out energy at their edges. He saw in the American village, especially, the betraying signs of a civilization perpetually overreaching itself and obliged to surrender again and again to nature all it had gained. "How many thousand villages, frost-bitten, palsied, full of a morbid, bloodless death-in-life, villages that have lost, if they ever possessed, the secret of self-perpetuation, lie scattered across the continent!"

Before T. S. Eliot had symbolized contemporary civilization

as the wasteland, and before F. Scott Fitzgerald made similar symbolic use in *The Great Gatsby* of the huge ash heaps characteristically surrounding our cities, Brooks expressed his shock at realizing "that our Eastern villages, the seats of all the civilization we have, are themselves scarcely anything but the waste and ashes of pioneering." The sight of ancient Long Island villages, with their "crazy, weather-beaten houses . . . the rotting porches and the stench of decay that hangs about their walls, the weed-choked gardens, the insect-ridden fruit trees, the rusty litter along the roads, the gaunt, silent farmers who stalk by in the dusk" suggested, rather than argued didactically, how much the old American individualism, as seen in the remnants of its enterprising spirit scattered over the landscape, had now become ineffectual.

Brooks saw the same symbolic meaning in the American personalities he had encountered. Before Hemingway did, he noted the paradox of the American "boy-man." In a company of American Rhodes scholars Brooks had met "pallid and wizened, little old men . . . rather stale and flat and dry." He remembered "this professor and that" and "how thin, how deficient in the tang and buoyancy of youth, in personal conviction and impassioned fancy" they had seemed. These characteristics were suggestive of the frigid quality of American intellectual and artistic life in general. "Serious people," he said, were really "like leaves prematurely detached from the great tree of life." But it was no less true of our men of action: "For if our old men of thought come to a standstill at middle age, our old men of action, as one sees them in offices, in the streets, in public positions, everywhere! are typically not old men at all but old boys." American life, at every level, seemed to Brooks to be in a "state of arrested development"; it had lost, if it had ever possessed, the principle of growth.

For Brooks, proof that American civilization lay poised in a state of arrested development—atrophied personality—was found in the myriad personalities engaged in the life of the mind and of art. Contemporary literature provided him with Theodore Dreiser's portraits of titans, financiers, and geniuses, with the whole community of frustrated and isolated souls found in Edgar Lee Masters' *Spoon River Anthology*. Side by side with his articles as they first appeared in the *Seven Arts* were the supporting portraits of the lost village souls in Sherwood Anderson's first

Winesburg, Ohio stories, along with those from other stories and poems which featured the same personality.

By and large this personality was still that of the Puritan, one visible, for example, in Brooks's description of "the old spiritual individualism" as "hard, stiff-necked, combative, opinionative, sectarian, self-willed, . . . the self-important monopolist of truth." He was still prone throughout these essays to reduce all explanations to the first cause of the Puritan. Increasingly, however, he began to blend the profile of the Puritan with that of the Pioneer—to speak, for example, of the "old materialistic individualism" of the Pioneer as "blood-brother" of the "old spiritual individualism." Puritanism, he asserted, was "a complete philosophy for the pioneer and by making human nature contemptible and putting to shame the charms of life it unleashed the acquisitive instincts of men, disembarrassing those instincts by creating the belief that the life of the spirit is altogether a secret life and that the imagination ought never to conflict with the law of the tribe."

Here, of course, he expressed another variation on his Highbrow, Lowbrow thesis. And, as in *America's Coming-of-Age,* he chastised Longfellow and Lowell for their lullabies to the "tired 'pioneer,' forerunner of the 'tired business man.'" Again he qualified Whitman's role in releasing the creative faculties of the American mind, because he too had shared the naive pioneer nature and had, in his declining years, purred like a cat in his satisfaction with material facts. Brooks easily used Howells' famous utterance about the American novelist recording only the more American "smiling aspects of life," and called it a "declaration of artistic bankruptcy." American writers generally were "victims of the universal taboo which the ideal of material success, of the acquisitive life, has placed upon experience." It did not matter that these writers often were of the finest artistic conscience. They had been taught too long "to repress everything that conflicts with the material welfare of their environment," and their environment provided so little nourishment for the imagination "that they do not so much mature at all as externalize themselves in a world of externalities."

The task of criticism and philosophy should have been to create an intellectual situation which the creative energy of Young America could have used. But the critics and philosophers had failed, according to Brooks; and in the sharpest language he had yet employed, he suggested why. "Our Critics" had all the satiric thrust of Brooks's earlier demolition of "Our Poets," sharper perhaps because the worthies on whom he loosed his irony (Babbitt, Brownell, More, Sherman, Spingarn, and others) were still very much alive. Indeed, almost every one of the critics he named had recently scolded the younger generation. Brooks's essay consequently had the special flavor of a youth's defiance of his elders. The timing of his essay also added a note of anguished bafflement, for it first appeared in the *Seven Arts* in May, 1917, during the dark moments of the first weeks of America's entry into the European war. Brooks's angry tones of bewilderment expressed for most of the magazine's staff and contributors the conviction, as he put it, that they had "witnessed the failure and breakdown of intellectualism itself."

There was irony in his casting in the face of these critics their own favorite touchstone, Matthew Arnold, and his remark that it is "the business of the critical power to see the object as in itself it really is." In doing this, Brooks said, the critics had failed. Far from seeing "the object as in itself it really is," they did not see at all "the object, the supreme object, America, the living creative life of America." Later, in a revision of this essay Brooks added that these older critics had not "observed the conditions that hamper and enfeeble [the creative life]. Consequently, they have not been able to stimulate and focus it."[4] The addition illumines Brooks's estimate of his own role and function at that point in his career.

The irony of Brooks's charge was twofold, however, for his essay made it quite clear that the critics themselves had weakened the creative life:

> That is only natural perhaps in the pundits of our criticism, Paul Elmer More and Irving Babbitt, for example, who feel that there is little worth seeing in a world Rousseau has perverted. And perhaps it is not surprising in such sensitive minds of the older generation as Mr. Brownell and Mr. Woodberry, who responded so passionately in their youth to visions of grace that never could have been ours, that they have no heart for the homelier tasks of America. But, remarkably, it is just as true of those more complacent and sometimes all too complacent critics of the middle generation who feel themselves in life apparently

by no means alien to the stirring American scene. Interest, mere
friendly interest, for severe interest we cannot expect, is the last
boon our critics yield us. Is it strange, then, that our creative
life halts and stammers in bewilderment? (127)

In this passage, a revision of the original essay in which Brooks
had attacked particular members of the middle generation, he
deleted his earlier references to Joel E. Spingarn and Stuart P.
Sherman, for in the interim he had achieved a rapprochement
with them. But for the others—Babbitt, More, Brownell—he let
his words stand. None of them had been able to descend "into
the thick of reality," as Lessing had done for the German character, or as Sainte-Beuve, perpetuating an inherited organic culture, had done for the French. Unlike these European critics,
the American critics possessed no sympathy for the creative life
of their contemporaries. Brooks accused them of being "incredulous pedagogues by necessity . . . driven to destroy in others the
poet that has died in themselves." This comment would have to
be, as Brooks put it, "the merciful epitaph" of their humanism.[5]
And so it remained for at least a decade until Paul Elmer More
launched a new Shelburne Series (1928) directly attacking the
contemporary naturalistic writing, and Norman Foerster revived
the whole controversy with his collection of essays by Babbitt,
More, and others in *Humanism in America* (1930).

Norman Foerster's role was an important one, both in reviving
interest in the humanist position and, through his books (*Toward
Standards, Criticism in America*) and a widely adopted anthology
of American literature, in extending and rehabilitating humanist
judgments of literature after the smoke of battle had cleared.
Yet, there had been one brief moment when he might have been
swayed to support the radicalism of Brooks. From the University
of North Carolina, where he was then a young professor of English, he wrote to Brooks and told him how much *Letters and
Leadership* had excited him and other members of his depart-
ment. Brooks's statement of the American literary situation
seemed right and "very fine" to Foerster, but he was puzzled as
to what Brooks called for in its place and how whatever this
was could be secured. He understood the More-Babbitt-Sherman
school, he said; but he wished Brooks would help him understand
the new school.[6]

Foerster's enthusiasm, coupled with his plea, reveals the kind of impact Brooks's book made upon discerning minds of the younger generation. With his diagnosis of what ailed America there was general agreement, in fact enthusiastic agreement. Brooks expressed for other young men their own sense of the American malady. What's more, they wholeheartedly approved his insistence that it was they, Young America, who occupied the center of hope. But they were puzzled, as Foerster was, about where they should attach their desire when, as Brooks made all too clear, there was so little in America that was lovable.

Part of their puzzlement stemmed from the ambivalence in Brooks's attack on the pragmatists in "Our Awakeners," the last of his *Seven Arts* articles. The confusion was a consequence of the abstract language, highly charged though it was, to which Brooks resorted when he touched upon the signs of renaissance, the faint evidence he detected that the "race of artists" he called for was coming into its own.

"Pragmatism has failed us," said Brooks, "because it has attempted to fill the place that only a national poetry can adequately fill." Brooks would not deny that both William James and John Dewey were better called poets than philosophers; he complained, however, that "they were not *sufficiently* poets to intensify the conception of human nature that they had inherited from our tradition. . . ." They had enthroned "the intelligence which merely sees, in place of the imagination which sees and feels"; consequently, they had sanctioned the American habit of treating life as a mechanism in which efficiency became an end in itself.

On this theme Brooks was back to a point he had started from in *The Wine of the Puritans;* he was objecting to the idea of a mechanistic universe. But he was not very successful in creating an organically conceived alternative. He deferred to European thinkers—to Goethe, to Ruskin and William Morris, to Shaw and H. G. Wells—and to what he called the "dynamic personal terms" with which each had embraced the life of Europe. In "Towards the Future," he called for an intellectual life in America "sustained by the emotional life," as, he argued, it had been true in Europe. But the nearest he came to announcing a program was in demanding "a class," one like the student class of Europe, "united in a common discipline and forming a sort of natural breeding ground for the leadership that we desire."

Here he pointed to the signs of the coming into existence of such a class—chiefly the evidence of "desire" among young Americans, a desire awakened by the war, by their experiences of travel and study abroad, by the examples of the reborn nationalities elsewhere. These were "reborn not to the greater glory of imperialism but in the name of an incalculably rich international humanity that beckons from the future . . . ." Idealistic and emotionally appealing as this desire is, Norman Foerster's puzzlement is understandable.

With Brooks's own friends and with his *Seven Arts* associates, he had closer rapport, however; and it was chiefly for them that he spoke of "desire" for a new synthesis in American life. Randolph Bourne, Waldo Frank, and Sherwood Anderson shared with Brooks the same passion and expressed it in the same language—for Frank and Anderson often spoke almost with idolatry of Brooks, calling him, in Anderson's phrase, "an inciter of flame." Bourne, having committed himself more deeply as a disciple to John Dewey, suffered deeper pangs of betrayal at pragmatism's "failure" and understood better than the others Brooks's rejection of the "awakeners." Certainly, in the essays Bourne wrote for the final numbers of the *Seven Arts*, he went far beyond Brooks in his ironic analysis of intellectualism's failure.

Perhaps even better than Brooks, Bourne divined the kind of leadership which a younger generation, disillusioned with liberalism, would follow in the postwar years. Writing to Brooks on the eve of the publication of *Letters and Leadership*, Bourne predicted that "our sense of leadership would come from discontent, from the intolerable feeling that we are alien in a world that no one around us is trying with intelligent fervor to set right." What the younger generation wanted, Bourne continued —and here he nicely summed up Brooks's position—was an idealism not full of compromises, but one that was more concerned with "American civilization than with American politics," that had more interest for "American life, liberty and the pursuit of happiness than for a model constitution and a watertight political-democratic system."

These malcontents—those who were disenchanted with the political liberalism which the war had shown up—were, Bourne maintained, the ones who would respond to the kind of leadership Brooks offered. He had some notions, he told Brooks, "of how that leadership could be created. . . . I imagine people must be appealed to to desire things mightily." But what was the "technique" Brooks had in mind? Had he a plan?[7]

The puzzlement was not Foerster's alone or Bourne's. It may even have extended to Brooks. He had been pressed by his friends to come forth with a program. So, in the preface he added to *Letters and Leadership* he said that he hoped one would be found "between the lines." But he must have known that although much hope and desire came out of his lines, of a technique for the future there was nothing.

Brooks was not, however, without a personal program. His critics and his friends, in demanding a technique of him, overlooked his stated function of himself as critic: to make an intellectual situation from which the creative power could profit. Toward this end he had taken a long stride with *America's Coming-of-Age, Letters and Leadership,* and his needling role in the *Seven Arts;* he had succeeded in making a generation of American writers highly self-conscious about America. He had pointed out the tensions and contradictions in the world that they must shape and give expression to.

But how to make malleable for art the bewildering diversity of the American experience had been, and remains, a central problem of the American artist. In weaving together the strands of Puritanism, industrialism, pioneering, humanism, and pragmatism, and the fibrous threads that cling to each of these traditions in American life, Brooks provided a patterned background against which writers could cast their own visions. In calling them to do just this, he bestowed upon them the highest of responsibilities: to create a civilization as they would a work of art. In ways perhaps too intangible to measure, as Randolph Bourne predicted they would be, Brooks's leadership asserted itself. He had called for a new class of writers, and they responded and turned to him. But he had to lead, thereafter, in his own way.

CHAPTER 5

The Search for a Usable Past

THE YEARS immediately following World War I contained a bewildering mixture of attitudes, feelings, and ideas. The high-sounding note of idealism on which Americans had gone to war lingered for a while, but it had more and more the hollowness of mockery in it. After Versailles, Americans did not abandon idealism so much as they narrowed its focus, directing it back upon themselves; they were determined that if they could not make the world safe for democracy, America would at least be made safe for Americans. The rush "back to normalcy" was a reaction, and often a reactionary one; but for some Americans the war's end meant a return to abandoned or interrupted plans, projects, and hopes for America's reform. Van Wyck Brooks was one of these men, an idealist still, but no reactionary.

Much had occurred, however, to dampen his hopes, to sadden and make wistful his dream of an America coming of age. The satiric drive of his prewar writing and the disdainful outbursts of indignation at the American scene had been buoyant on a wave of creative energy. But the war had thwarted, cast aside, and misdirected much of that energy. The *Seven Arts,* uncompromising in its anti-war policy, had backed Randolph Bourne by publishing his scathing analysis of the "war-technique," his scourge of the intellectuals for their failure to keep America out of war, and his call for a resurgence of "malcontentedness" as the only way to keep alive America's promise. Brooks, agreeing with Bourne, had nevertheless dissented with the other editors' decision to carry the magazine into politics, beyond its role as defender of the arts, lest it be scuttled in the process. All too soon his fears were confirmed. The magazine's sponsors withdrew their support; and, despite an ardent appeal for subscribers assistance, the issue of October, 1917, ended the *Seven Arts.* The bright promising venture closed, a victim of war-hysteria or, as Bourne had called it earlier, of the Puritans' will to power.

The next year, shortly after the Armistice, Bourne himself died of pneumonia; and in a short while legend had made him another martyr of the war. Brooks's memorial tribute to his friend, which introduced a posthumous collection of Bourne's essays, *The History of a Literary Radical* (1920), contributed much to his canonization. Brooks cast him as the younger generation's first spokesman, as "the new America incarnate." In reviewing his friend's desires for America and in speaking of his own, Brooks revealed the depths of his indebtedness to Bourne. He saw in his personal loss a national tragedy as well, and the shock of Bourne's death added to his postwar despair.

Up to this point, except as it may have reflected his own uncertainties, the theme of the interrupted, unfulfilled, and frustrated career had been for Brooks largely a product of his reading. His close association with Bourne, however, added a very personal dimension to his concern for the fate of the writer in America. The indebtedness to Bourne in this respect may be measured in the tones that darkened three of Brooks's major post-war writings: *The Ordeal of Mark Twain* (1920), "The Literary Life in America" (1921), and *The Pilgrimage of Henry James* (1925).

I *Mark Twain*

The posthumous publication of Twain's *The Mysterious Stranger* (1910) and A. B. Paine's two volumes of Twain's *Letters* (1917) had renewed interest in the American humorist. The first came as something of a shock to those who had not suspected the undercurrent of pessimism in Twain's works, and Mencken had seized upon this book as evidence of the thwarted artist in Twain, a situation "highly suggestive" to Mencken of Puritanism's baleful influence on American letters. Stuart Sherman, expectedly taking an opposite course, had praised Twain for his unflinching assertion of "the ordinary self of the ordinary American."

Brooks's friends eagerly anticipated his setting both of these critics straight. Bourne had written that he "chortled with joy" at how much Brooks was going to show up Sherman. Waldo Frank, in the midst of writing his own book, *Our America* (1919), addressed Brooks during the first few days of relief and exhilaration at the war's end: "We must have Mark Twain before long. Do you not feel that with the ending of the butchery in Europe, the sun of our generation dawned over the rim of the world?"[1]

Frank's *Our America* preceded Brooks's *Ordeal* by only a few months, appearing in November, 1919, while the latter was published in April, 1920. It was patently indebted to both Brooks and Bourne in its exploiting of the theme of Puritanism, and in being about an America still in the throes of an age of pioneering, now possessed by industrialism. It differed from Brooks's early work, however, in its apocalyptic spirit and tone which were peculiarly Frank's own, and also in its addiction to the language and scheme of Freudian and Jungian psychology. In this respect, the indebtedness lies in the other direction, for Frank, along with Bourne, and perhaps James Oppenheim, were Brooks's tutors. It was Waldo Frank who first suggested that Mark Twain's life and work (with the exception of *Huckleberry Finn*) had been a betrayal of Twain's artistic soul, a retreat behind "the dikes of social inhibition and intellectual fear." And this was essentially the thesis Brooks gave to a startled American public in his *The Ordeal of Mark Twain*.

The rash hypothesis is no less startling today, when Mark Twain's reputation as one of America's first-rank writers is even more firmly secured by the weight of a half-century of scholarship and criticism than it was in the decade after his death when it appeared inflated by the first outpourings of eulogies. But to read *The Ordeal of Mark Twain* again, as a fable of the dilemma of the American writer, as a case study of the plight of the artist in the modern world, is to find it still startlingly timely. For the modern artist, if he is to keep and sustain the integrity that supports his vision, must be ever alert to the obstacles that an a-cultural society sets before him. And that society, in turn, so pragmatic in every other way, has still to learn something of the care and feeding of its creative talents.

Brooks stated his thesis boldly and firmly in the early pages of his book. The reasons for Mark Twain's pessimism, only recently revealed and a matter of some speculation, were not hard to surmise:

> It is an established fact, if I am not mistaken, that these morbid feelings of sin, which have no evident cause, are the result of having transgressed some inalienable life-demand peculiar to one's nature. It is as old as Milton that there are talents which are

"death to hide," and I suggest that Mark Twain's "talent" was just so hidden. That bitterness of his was the effect of a certain miscarriage in his creative life, a balked personality, and arrested development of which he was himself almost wholly unaware, but which for him destroyed the meaning of life. The spirit of the artist in him, like the genie at last released from the bottle, overspread in a gloomy vapour the mind it had never quite been able to possess. (25)

With the manner and tone of a prosecuting attorney—a similarity that occurred to many reviewers—Brooks delivered his summation of this thesis in the ten chapters that followed. He documented it with the evidence he found in Twain's life and work on the one hand, and in the epoch and society within which Twain had lived and worked on the other. In the interaction that he distinguished between the life and the times, he sketched a portrait of the archetypal American artist.

Not to see that Mark Twain figures throughout Brooks's book as an emblem of the creative spirit in America is to miss the "method" behind Brooks's emphatic disappointment at Twain's failure to sustain the supreme genius he was born to be. That "method" had become Brooks's habit of seeing America itself in terms of personality. *The Ordeal of Mark Twain* is a sustained analogy, therefore, between the personality of the artist (Mark Twain) and that of America. The study of Twain was also one of America in its adolescence, not yet fulfilling its promise. The motive of the book was that of *America's Coming-of-Age:* to announce that the period of adolescence was past. Mark Twain had been "the supreme victim of an epoch in American history, an epoch that has closed."

Brooks concluded by asking: "Has the American writer of today the same excuse for missing his vocation? Not if he reads the driven, disenchanted faces of his more sensitive countrymen, not if he remembers the splendid part his confrères have played in the human drama of other times and other peoples, and asks himself whether the hour has not come to put away childish things and walk the stage as poets do" (256). This statement surely underscores the exhortatory intention of the book. Brooks might have chosen another literary figure to illustrate the same thesis; but he could hardly have chosen a better one than Mark Twain who so blatantly combined the Philistine and the artist.

In his estimate of Twain, Brooks was admittedly one-sided.

He turned every detail of his life and works to illustrate the thesis of the balked and divided artist. Part of the book's force lies in the sheer mass of this kind of detail, though any one detail, taken out of context, easily makes Brooks appear to be thesis-mongering—as some reviewers charged. One wants to protest, perhaps, when Brooks pounces upon Twain's notorious absentmindedness as evidence of the artist's unconscious rebellion against the demands and incursions upon his calling. Yet this detail *is* an isolated one. Brooks's severe indictment of Twain's lapses from artistic integrity rests upon the way he marshaled this damning trait along with a host of others: the sardonic record of Twain's latter days; Twain's constant harking back to his years as a Mississippi River pilot; the signs of a neurotic childhood; his desire to succeed as a man of business; his remonstrances against the genteel strictures of his wife's society (and his yielding to them); his lack of courage in abandoning (with others) the dinner organized for Maxim Gorky, and so on. The full catalogue of Brooks's brief, taken as a whole, remains persuasive.

Though Brooks's tone often suggests otherwise, he wrote of Twain more in sorrow than in anger. Stern though his rebuke was, he did not altogether ignore Twain's accomplishments. True, one might wish, as Waldo Frank did, that Brooks had expanded more upon the "supremacy" he gave to *Huckleberry Finn*. Yet the measure of a critic's judgment can not rest merely on how long he dwells upon his subject. Brooks did concede the triumph of *Huckleberry Finn* and, moreover, explained it in a way that has proved highly suggestive since other critics have picked it up and explored it: when Twain found the right "mask" and created the right narrative voice through which he could speak, "he let all the cats out of the bag," and his irony took shape through the interplay of his own voice and that of his narrator.

The book, of course, was not about Twain's triumph but about his "ordeal"—why and where Twain had gone wrong after *Huckleberry Finn*. There were plenty of others, like Stuart Sherman, who would make him out to be "The Great Man," by calling him "the typical American"—thus flattering every American. Brooks sought to rescue Twain from that fate, to get writers to face up to themselves, to get Americans generally to examine the sources of their self-complacency. If Mark Twain's story was part of the prose Odyssey of the American people, as Stuart Sherman asserted, then it was not a usable tradition for the modern artist. Its prose had sterilized, rather than promoted, the creative impulses of the individual.

When Brooks scourged the pioneering tradition and the business civilization which was an extension of it with the intent of shattering American complacency about the past, he was simply elaborating on themes he had expressed before. Notably, however, he played down the animus against Puritanism which had dominated his earlier books. The Calvinistic tradition incarnate in Twain's mother and an occasional reference to Twain's wife and "all those other narrow, puritanical influences to which he had subjected himself," or to the Puritanic-commercialism of the Gilded Age—these are the few direct references to Puritanism.

Possibly this reduction to a minor key may have been influenced by Randolph Bourne. Amused at the spectacle of Mencken and Sherman clashing over the issue of Puritanism, Bourne had, in effect, called for a moratorium; he had announced the "Puritan" to be a straw man and the "real enemy" to be the genteel tradition.[2] At any rate, Brooks gave over one whole chapter to Twain as "A Candidate for Gentility." The onus against the Pioneer was early linked in his mind with the Puritan; the shift was, therefore, more one in terms than in targets. In making Twain a symbol of balked creative life in America, Brooks tried to show that "in his dominant character Mark Twain had become the archetypal pioneer," "the typical American magnate," and "the spokesman of the Philistine majority." But Twain's "essential instinct, the instinct of the artist," was "naturally in opposition" to all these poses forced upon him by "a sort of unconscious conspiracy [that] actuated all America against the creative life."

In order to project Twain as the pioneer and businessman (in whom the poet was lost) Brooks drew heavily upon Herbert Croly's *The Promise of American Life* (1909), a book which had served as a kind of primer of rhetoric for young intellectuals of the Progressive movement. Croly had argued that pioneer democracy had held individuality suspect, subtly pressing everyone into a common mold. Similarly, he had argued that businessmen compromised their individualism as much through success as through failure since "the ultimate measure of the value of their work is the same, and is nothing but its results in cash."

Brooks showed how Twain illustrated both arguments, writing in the chapter "The Gilded Age" one of the most stringent analyses of American society's materialistic standards of success since Twain's own novel of the same title. Brooks's portrait presented a balked, self-deluded personality, an outer façade of successful appearance hiding an inner despair:

> Was America really happier, during the Gilded Age, than any other nation? It was a dark jumble of decayed faiths, of unconfessed class distinctions, of repressed desires, of inarticulate misery —witness *The Story of a Country Town* and *A Son of the Middle Border* and *Ethan Frome;* but to have said so would have "hurt business." The jolly family party was open, after all, to very few and those, moreover, who, except for their intense family affections and a certain joy of action, had foregone the best things that life has to offer. But was it not perhaps for the welfare of all that they so diligently promulgated the myth of America's "manifest destiny"? Perhaps, since the prodigious task of pioneering had to be carried through. Perhaps also because, after the disillusionments of the present epoch, that myth will prove to have had, in spite of all, a certain beautiful residuum of truth. (79)

Much has been made of the fact that *The Ordeal of Mark Twain* was a pioneer study of a literary personality in its use of the insights of psychoanalysis—particularly those of Freud. Frederick J. Hoffman has shown, however, that by 1915 psychoanalysis was "fairly well launched in the magazines from which the intellectual of that day drew his information," and Freud's ideas were widely discussed.[3] By 1920 Brooks could confidently assume an easy familiarity with those ideas on the part of the intellectuals he addressed, particularly the writers. Although it broke no new ground, Brooks's book pioneered nevertheless as one of the first major works to use some psychoanalytic terms to explore a major literary personality.

Actually, after due note is made of how Brooks used psychoanalytic terms, it is misleading to describe *The Ordeal of Mark Twain* as a contribution to Freudian criticism, whatever priority one may claim for it. In fact, in a review of Katherine Anthony's *Margaret Fuller: A Psychological Biography*, Brooks revealed his own reservations about the usefulness of psychoanalysis applied to biography. Psychoanalysis at best, he said, could have only clinical value in providing some explanation of causes. "What counts in biography," he said in a *Freeman* essay, "is not the causes of the character but the significance of the character itself, or rather, since the biographer is of equal importance with the subject, the impact of one character on another."[4] This statement can stand as Brooks's explanation of his intention to show the significance of Mark Twain to his generation.

Since he drew two portraits of personalities, one of Twain and one of America, and assumed in each some "malady of the soul" whose nature he sought to explain, Brooks laced his diction liberally with the many terms about the unfulfilled person that were available to him. Many of these came from the glossary of psychoanalysis, but just as many came from the discussion about the personality, especially the two-sided personality, which was given to the public domain by nineteenth-century romanticism. From the same vast domain he drew words like "soul," phrases like "inner-life" and, above all, "free-will" and "creative-will"— concepts which psychoanalysis steadfastly avoided. These terms, in fact, rather than the loosely employed psychoanalytic diction, point to the real source of his method—the romantics' concern for the psyche, not the psychoanalysts' concern for the id.

Moreover, Brooks's preoccupation with the malady of the ideal, with the sensitive soul that cringed before the demands of a crude material order, for all its roots in romantic literature, had become peculiarly his own property. He had arrived at a meaning for repression—both of the individual artist, Twain, and of America—before the term had been given new currency. The metaphor he used in stating his thesis—"the spirit of the artist in [Twain], like the genie at last released from the bottle, overspread in a gloomy vapour the mind it had never quite been able to possess"—had its paternity not in Freud but in his own early book, *The Wine of the Puritans.*

That he should have used psychoanalytic language at all is explained finally by recalling the polemical intent of the book. It made use, therefore, of the rhetoric that was current. It used Freud, as it used Herbert Croly: metaphorically. Brooks argued after the manner of the artist, analogically, not psychologically. His readers got the point. "The climate of literature seemed different after Brooks had spoken," Malcolm Cowley has testified. "He had given courage to at least a few writers, and courage is hardly less contagious than fear." *The Ordeal of Mark Twain* was, as one reviewer named it, "an American morality," a fable for every American, and specifically for every one who would be a writer.[5]

The Ordeal of Mark Twain set off a controversy that still continues. The reasons are not far to seek. Brooks offended on several counts: he transformed a national idol into a tragic figure but without sufficient redemption to make him nobly tragic; he offended proprieties in the pairing of Twain's mother and wife as villains; he challenged the myth about the West and the nation's golden past of pioneering, particularly the myth of the rural paradise in the American village; and he assailed the dream of success in a business civilization. Calculated, in its dogmatic and assertive tone, to stir debate, it succeeded eminently. The story of its criticism by others is a long chapter in the history of Mark Twain scholarship and in the reassessments still going on of the American frontier and America's business civilization.[6]

Bernard De Voto in *Mark Twain's America* (1932) assaulted Brooks thoroughly, and he flatly concluded that Brooks was not qualified to report and pass judgment on Twain. Brooks had erred, De Voto maintained, because of his gross ignorance of the frontier traditions that had produced Twain and because of his habit of converting everything into the data of psychoanalysis. De Voto professed puzzlement at the "possibly mystical meaning" Brooks found in words like "the creative process," and he was especially grieved that Brooks's thesis commanded so much prestige that it was advanced and reiterated by other critics after him, like Lewis Mumford and Matthew Josephson.

When Brooks got to a revised edition in 1933 he softened a phrase or two, eliminated an outburst against New England, but altered his essential thesis not one bit. More than once after that, however, he expressed regret that he had not sung more the praises of *Huckleberry Finn,* as Sherwood Anderson had urged. He even confessed that the "psychologist [had] inhibited the past in me."[7] He redressed the balance, when he wrote his chapter on Mark Twain for *The Times of Melville and Whitman* (1947). Carefully he demonstrated his appreciation of Twain's humor and of Twain's "masterly grasp" of the American scene in *Roughing It.* He allowed the poet in himself to expand on *Huckleberry Finn* and on Mark Twain, "the serio-comic Homer of this old primitive Western world, its first pathfinder in letters, its historian and poet." Yet, in his more recent memoirs (*Days* of the Phoenix), he affirmed that though he saw clearly the objections made to his *Ordeal,* he "still felt [Twain] had made the great refusal and that *The Ordeal of Mark Twain* was substantially just." Perhaps, he added, he might have presented "only half of the real Mark Twain but certainly much, if not the whole, of a well-known abstract character, the typical American author as we knew him at the moment."[8]

II   *The Literary Life*

A year after publishing his *Ordeal,* Brooks wrote the essay "The Literary Life in America," his contribution to the notoriously despairing symposium, *Civilization in the United States* (1922), edited by Harold Stearns. Parts of this essay had first appeared in Brooks's column "A Reviewer's Notebook" in the *Freeman* (May 25, 1921). In that essay, after asserting that in America the literary scene presented the spectacle of one long list of spiritual casualties, a chronic state where youthful promise was never redeemed, he picked up again an image he had applied to Mark Twain as a "shorn Samson":

> This being so, how much one would like to assume, with certain of our critics, that the American writer is a sort of Samson bound with the brass fetters of the Philistines and requiring only to have those fetters cast off in order to be able to conquer the world! That, as I understand it, is the position of Theodore Dreiser, who recently remarked of certain of our novelists: "They succeeded in writing but one book before the iron hand of convention took hold of them." There is this to be said for the argument, that if the American writer as a type shows less resistance than the European writer it is plainly because he has been insufficiently equipped, stimulated, nourished by the society into which he has been born. . . . But what is significant is that the American writer *does* show less resistance; and as literature is nothing but the expression of power, of the creative will, of "free will," in short, is it not more accurate to say, not that the "iron hand of convention" takes hold of our writers, but that our writers yield to the "iron hand of convention"? Samson had lost his virility before the Philistines bound him; it was because he had lost his virility that the Philistines were able to bind him. The American writer who "goes wrong" is in a similar case.[9]

That "well known abstract character," the American writer, a Samson shorn because of a failure of the will, bothered Brooks; in fact, he became something of an obsession with him. And the nervous collapse he suffered at the end of the decade could indicate that Brooks was projecting his own fears and doubts about his own career. In his memoirs he spoke candidly of his "season in hell," strongly suggesting that he had succumbed to the fear that he had "gone wrong." He suffered the anguish of a divided self, discovering that he "had always worked by following [his] nose . . . had never been able to think anything out but rather *felt* things out in cumbersome fashion . . . writing always intuitively. . . ."

This candor does with some fairness describe the emotional fervor marking the writing of his early years. His statement is even suggestive of the sources of that special doubleness of vision in his writing from *The Wine of the Puritans* through *The Pilgrimage of Henry James;* of the frequent presence of two narrative voices, one a Jeremiah, the other from Ecclesiastes; or even of the invention of an alter ego, as in *The Wine,* or of "Henry Wickford," who signed the *Freeman* column which grew into the essay on "The Literary Life in America." Nevertheless, the feelings Brooks articulated were genuine and his intuitions sound; indeed, most of his contemporaries shared and corroborated them. If he spoke from some sense of personal malaise, it was also that of a whole generation.

Moreover, his writing in these years was not without rational design and purpose. To make an intellectual situation that writers could use had been the job he had assigned himself. In large measure his polemical criticism had done just that. Among writers, a full-scale self-examination was on, and Brooks was at its center. One purpose of that criticism he had announced in his essay "On Creating a Usable Past," written and published in the *Dial* while America was still at war. The present was a void, he said, one in which the "American writer floats . . . because the past that survives . . . is . . . without living value." This past, however, was censored by the commercial and moralistic mind of the older generation, the professors; and it was not the only possible past.

We can and must, Brooks asserted, "discover, invent a usable past . . . that is what a vital criticism always does."[10] We must take from the past "what is important for us," approaching it "personally," with full awareness of the shortcomings and anarchy of present literary life. *The Ordeal of Mark Twain* had been the first full step toward that end. Only in that sense had he "personally" confronted Twain to discover the "significance" of the impact of Twain's character upon himself, writing in a different age. "The Literary Life in America" addressed itself to the anarchy of the contemporary American environment where "everything . . . it goes without saying, tends to repress the creative and to stimulate the competitive impulses."

The essay also hit hard at a second purpose in Brooks's work, announced first in *Letters and Leadership,* and closely related to his first: the need for critics to respect themselves by feeling that what they did mattered, that they were working in a great line, that they were of a "school": "The successful pursuit of the ego is what makes literature; this requires not only a certain inner intensity but also a certain courage, and it is doubtful whether, in any nation, any considerable number of men can summon up that courage and maintain it unless they have *seen the thing done.*" In many ways Brooks devoted his energy, in an age of reaction, to stirring "the few into a consciousness of themselves." *The Ordeal* had firmly established him as a reputable critic and placed him very much in the center of the post-war literary world. He knew the literary life in America.

He spent his days with writers and artists. Westport, Connecticut, and the surrounding area—a short drive beyond New York City, where Brooks lived—became an "archetype of exurbia," something of a colony for writers, artists, and intellectuals. But for the next four years after *The Ordeal of Mark Twain* he spent two or three days a week in New York City in the offices of the *Freeman,* whose staff he had joined as an associate editor. To the *Freeman,* a somewhat more sober *Seven Arts,* Brooks contributed a weekly column, "A Reviewer's Notebook," throughout most of its four lively years (except for a period of six months when he was on leave, writing his *James* book). In its pages he worked at stirring the critical scene by hitting regularly at his two themes—the creation of a usable past, and the need for writers to respect their integrity as writers. He met most of the critical issues of the day and created a few of his own.

As the editor who was chiefly in charge of the *Freeman's* literary policy, Brooks cultivated and taught the craft of reviewing to the new writers he recruited for the magazine. In the

Freeman offices he first met Malcolm Cowley, Matthew Josephson, and Lewis Mumford who came nearest to filling the place
of friendship left empty by Randolph Bourne. Just down the
street from the *Freeman,* the rejuvenated *Dial* had its offices,
and sooner or later Brooks met most of the contributors to both
magazines—John Dos Passos, Newton Arvin, Edmund Wilson,
William Carlos Williams, E. E. Cummings, Marianne Moore,
and many others.

To many of these writers, Brooks had become a kind of sage.
He impressed them with his vast store of information about
American literature. He was full of ideas, suggestions for articles
and books, and he frequently paved the way to publication. Had
he been vested in academic robes he could hardly have played
better the role of dissertation supervisor, for he inspired and
encouraged studies like Lewis Mumford's *The Golden Day: A
Study in American Literature and Culture* (1926) and his biography, *Herman Melville* (1929); Matthew Josephson's *Portrait
of the Artist as American* (1930); and Constance Rourke's *The
Roots of American Culture* (1942).

Brooks made constant plans to widen the discussion of literature in America and to create an audience, an "intellectual situation," for writers. In 1921 with Lewis Mumford and Walter
Fuller, he discussed a proposal to issue a series of paperbacks,
a project which, after some metamorphoses, realized itself in
the Literary Guild. Appropriately, the first Literary Guild selection was yet another Brooks project: *The American Caravan*
(1927), a yearbook "conducted by literary men in the interests
of a growing American literature," which he edited with Mumford, Alfred Kreymborg, and Paul Rosenfeld. The *Freeman* had
opened its columns to Harold Stearns, with whom Brooks worked
in the planning of that inquiry into *Civilization in the United
States.*

With Joel Spingarn Brooks talked over proposals for certain
joint tasks since, as Spingarn wrote, "Both of us agree that a
renovation of American criticism (a reinvigoration of literary
ideas through a clearer understanding of the meaning of criticism and literary history) is one of the essentials of American
life."[11] Spingarn's *Criticism in America: Its Function and Status*
(1924), a collection of recent critical essays, including one by
Brooks, was one of the fruits of these plans.

His discussions with Spingarn carried over into print, as each critic, while respecting the other, sharpened his point of view on the question of the critic's function in America, and to some extent they reached a mild agreement. Spingarn reiterated his insistence that no critic in America was prepared for "this day of battle" without some training in esthetic thinking, and he used the space offered him in the *Freeman* to lecture on the esthetic of Croce. But he also delivered "A New Manifesto" for the younger generation by saying that he who had once called upon young men for rebellion and doubt would now bring a halt to "Revolt for Revolt's sake"; he called instead for the exercise of a "creative will" and a new idealism. Brooks now found Spingarn's attitude a salutary one and conceded that "national consciousness is, in art, not an end but a means." He also agreed with Spingarn on the dangers of revolt for revolt's sake, pointing out, for instance, in the course of defending the petulant tone of much of the recent critical movement, that "the critical effort of the present generation will not begin to attain its object as long as it merely maddens people." With a sidewise glance at Mencken, he warned of the dangers of polemical criticism: "it tends to establish an orthodoxy of rebellion as complacent and stagnant as the established orthodoxy against which it rebels."

Conceding that his own kind of criticism merely led to the end Spingarn aimed at, and even that perhaps "the environment has received more than its due share of attention," Brooks inclined still to "demur" at the word "esthetic" and to reiterate in his turn that "it still remains for the critical faculty to make intellectual situations of which, as Arnold said, the creative power may properly avail itself." He repeated that "the main task of criticism in America remains rather social than aesthetic."

III *Expatriatism and Estheticism*

Brooks's main task, in fact, even while his left hand engaged in this kind of weekly refinement of his own critical position, was to coordinate these emphases with his right hand in a major demonstration of the danger to the artistic personality that divorced itself from its native social matrix. Almost as soon as he had completed his book on Twain, and coincident with his joining the *Freeman* staff, Brooks commenced the study that resulted in *The Pilgrimage of Henry James* (1925). Along with *The Or-*

deal of Mark Twain, this book became an important contribution to the postwar literary quarrels. Addressed, as was the first, to the contemporary scene, it was a calculated reply from the "middle generation" to the younger generation. Harold Stearns, spokesman for "the disillusioned young intellectuals," in an early issue of the *Freeman* presented the challenge: "We are cynical, and hateful, and rebellious, and materialistic. The only book that would interest us would be a book explaining why we should stay in America, when we have made enough money to get out." To check the tide of those like Stearns who seceded in distaste from the American scene, Brooks wrote *The Pilgrimage of Henry James.*

The themes of expatriatism and estheticism had preoccupied Brooks ever since *The Wine of the Puritans.* Except, however, for one allusion in *The Ordeal of Mark Twain,* where Brooks opposed the "true artist's [James] natural attitude towards his work" to Twain's lack of pride in his, Henry James figured nowhere in any of his earlier writing. His selection of James for his next "case-study" seems to have been dictated, at least in part, as with the Twain book, by the revival of interest in James brought about by posthumous comment and publications like *The Letters of Henry James* (1920). Brooks's *Freeman* review of the *Letters,* in fact, may be looked upon as "the germ" for *The Pilgrimage of Henry James.* He noted, for instance, that "one gathers there is to be no official biography," which was too bad; for the *Letters,* while revealing James as son, brother, or fellow artist, were wholly inadequate to the question of James "the man."

If this review marked the beginning of Brooks's study of James and announced his intention to illuminate "the man," subsequent *Freeman* articles written while he was engaged on the James book provide a running commentary on some of the contemporary literary issues he was trying to resolve in *The Pilgrimage of Henry James.* The plight of the American artist, his loneliness, the too frequent instances of his eclipsed genius, and the temptations he was prey to in a Puritanic-commercial environment— these themes recurred with increasing frequency in Brooks's *Freeman* column and were often linked to the subject and arguments of *The Pilgrimage of Henry James.* Ezra Pound, for instance, drew a high accolade from Brooks for having "very much at heart the civilization of these United States," for his performing a great service in "the pride with which he upholds the vocation of letters," and for his brilliant essay on Henry James.

At least two early versions of portions of *The Pilgrimage of Henry James* appeared first in Brooks's "Reviewer's Notebook" in the *Freeman*. These were specifically linked to the "question of the contemporary emigré" as raised by Harold Stearns in his *Freeman* articles on America and the Young Intellectuals. Brooks's alter ego, "Henry Wickford," spoke on another occasion of America's literature as flimsy because so little of it bore any "relation to the soil" because too many writers pursued only "sophistication"—one of the main charges Brooks finally leveled at Henry James. In an unsigned article Brooks addressed himself to the editors of the magazine *Secession,* agreeing with them that there was a good deal for our writers to secede from, but that they ought not therefore to retreat into concern only with "aesthetic problems." Expatriatism and estheticism thus became, for Brooks, nearly identical evils; each was a symptom of some failure of nerve.

At the same time that Brooks was experimenting with methods of revealing a literary personality, he paused to comment on the biographical efforts of others, and particularly upon the problems of American biography. Frequently, some of these comments reveal his own intentions in his biography. Raymond Weaver's biography of Melville, for instance, he found "too external," giving little of "the inner life of Melville," especially of the later Melville who had "continued to grow in his strange fashion, long after the eclipse of his talent." Or again he would remark (in a *Freeman* piece later republished as "Thoughts on Biography" in *Sketches in Criticism*) that it was the *significance* of the subject that was paramount in biography.

IV   *Henry James*

The Pilgrimage of Henry James was carefully prepared for, carefully and artfully written. Designed to present James "the man" and to reveal his "inner life," it sought also to expound his "significance," his symbolic importance to contemporary American writers. It searched a part of the American past for what could be used by writers in the present. Particularly, it was addressed to the postwar generation of writers who all too readily acquiesced in Brooks's judgment of the American en-

vironment and who wanted to know why they should not therefore secede—literally and imaginatively—to Europe and to Art.
Designed to provide an answer to this dilemma of the American
writer, the book paradoxically posed a dilemma for Brooks who
had not expected his fable of America to turn out so true.

Almost painfully Brooks had tried to refine his critical position
and to distinguish his point of view from those of other critics
with whom he otherwise shared a common desire. He took issue
with Mencken, who had joined him in the attack on Puritanic
America; and he shared nearly every point in Spingarn's program
of rebellion but dissented from his emphasis on estheticism. He
matched Ezra Pound in exhorting the writer to respect his craft
and to become a conscious member of a class, but he regretted
the "coteries" fostered by Pound. He had much in common with
Max Eastman's vision of a Socialist future, but he differed with
him strenuously on the role that writers and literature should
play in preparing for it. Moreover, too many of the younger
critics dismayed him, especially those who had derived from
his own books the very "fatalism" that he thought he had encouraged them to avoid.

The embarrassment and the pain are both evident in the
agonized style of the following passage from a *Freeman* column
written not long after he had had the chance to brood over the
reception of *The Ordeal of Mark Twain:*

> I say it with trepidation, lest the wrong people overhear me;
> but there have been too many complaints lately about the fate
> of the American writer. That the writer is not wanted in America,
> is not recognized in America, that our few great writers in the
> past have been chained and muzzled, that our few honest writers
> in the present are ignored, libelled and persecuted is an aspect
> of the truth for which there is much to be said; . . . that the
> American writer is usually a victim, in certain respects, of his
> environment, no one is going to deny. But he is a victim, it
> seems to me, less because his environment fails to appreciate
> him than because his environment fails to nourish him. And that
> is a very different thing. While America fails to nourish the
> writer, it appreciates the writer, on the whole, if he has been
> able, in spite of all, to make something of himself, almost, if not
> quite, in the measure of his deserts.[12]

Brooks effectively transcended the pain and anguish of his
personal dilemma as a critic in the creative effort of *The Pil-*

grimage of Henry James. Turning finally to the method as well as the intention of the fabulist, he wrote what was more nearly a novel; moreover, it was—as nearly every reviewer noted—a psychological novel in the manner of Henry James himself. A prefatory note frankly warned that Brooks had incorporated "many phrases and even longer passages" from James's writings, "usually without any indication of their sources." He said he resorted to this expedient "because he [knew] of no other means of conveying with strict accuracy at moments what he [conceived] to have been James's thoughts and feelings." The narrative voice was thus approximately that of James himself—as Brooks imagined it; but, of course, the final narrative voice was Brooks's.

The conception derived chiefly from James's autobiographical volumes, from his letters, and from the somewhat dangerous practice of making James's fictional characters speak for James himself. Finding a special affinity between his own past experiences and James's evocation of a past shining with his beloved "tiny particles" of memory, endlessly connected in a tightly woven tapestry of sense-images, Brooks in writing about James also wrote about himself—or rather about a destiny that might have been his had he yielded, as he contended James had done, to his enchanted "vision of Europe."

That it was partly Brooks's own story is more evident if we compare James's *A Small Boy and Others,* the first of James's three autobiographical volumes, with Brooks's first volume of memoirs, *Scenes and Portraits.* There are superficial resemblances, of course, in many memoirs by men of letters; but the shared pattern of these two books is a striking one and the comparison becomes significant when we note how the features of the childhood later recalled by Brooks were first read by him as those of the world in *A Small Boy and Others.*

In each memoir the writer shares and writes from the same sense of fascination with the "composition" he dimly perceives lurking in his own "story." Each writer has engaged his imagination with his memory; and, sharing the same impulse, each employs the same method of letting memory compose for him as he moves loosely through chronology. The present voice muses upon the innocence of a past fragment, then excitedly notes the "significance" which a yet later experience endowed the earlier, thereby giving it "connection." Of course, these are similarities James and Brooks share with others engaged in the remembrance of things past.

The real betrayal of James's impact on Brooks, however, lies in the pattern of the "world" each recalled: to James, it was "a small and compact and ingenuous society, screened in somehow conveniently from north and west, but open wide to the east." To Brooks, it was "a crowded little corner of the country, with windows opening towards Europe and closed towards the West." James sought, in part, to supply some justification for the "perversity" to which he confessed, that "sense of Europe" given him by his childhood world. Brooks's memoirs, noting his early involvement in a similarly patterned world, justified his subsequent reaction to it—to the "sense of America" which, it might well be said, became his "perversity."

There are other points of resemblance between these two remembered worlds by two men of letters of different yet overlapping generations, each trying to trace his America. The comparison helps in understanding *The Pilgrimage of Henry James* as, first of all, a creative dramatization of a direct meeting between two literary generations and between nineteenth-century America and twentieth-century America. *The Pilgrimage of Henry James* explored "the complex fate" of being an American, not alone of James, as he wrestled with his fate, but of Brooks. The battle which took place in Brooks himself, and the one which he also fought for his generation, was the one he attributed to James when James wrote: "one of the responsibilities [being an American] entails is fighting against a superstitious valuation of Europe."

Brooks argued that James had lost this fight. The world James had dreamed of entering, "the shimmering universe of the little boy on Fourteenth street," the world opening toward Europe, he had found. "He invented it—he discovered it, that is, for literature. He was the first to become conscious of an actual historic drama that has played its part in countless lives on the stage of two continents." Yet something of that boy's shimmering universe always persisted in the reality of the world James had invented. James's England, Brooks said, "was an idea, a veritable Platonic idea." His America, the "one of the two or three capital phases of the civilization of his country" which he knew "as no one else has known it," was real in somewhat the same way:

> Do not ask [James] if he knows the America that is rooted in the soil, the sober, laborious America of the pioneers, the dim unconscious, Titanic America that is taking shape in the darkness of the hinterland. His America, no less real, is that of the great towns of the Atlantic seaboard; it is, in particular, the America that lives in the thought, the memory, the expectation of the European world from which it has sprung. The nostalgia for the home of his ancestors of the American who has been liberated from the bondage of necessity, the romantic vision of the Old World that exists in the American heart, the drama of the émigré in search of the arts of life—this is his natural domain. He possesses it as truly as Balzac possessed the Paris of the Restoration. (93)

Of this world James was sure, Brooks said. So long as he retained "a vital connection with it"—with "his own race, even his own soil," which was his "Sacred Fount"—James had found in it abundant themes for tragedy, comedy, satire. His feeling for character, for human values in "the international situation," was right. This was the world in which he was "saturated"—the necessary condition, as James himself often said, for the novelist who would succeed.

But James chose continuous expatriation, grew increasingly remote from his roots in this world, and paid the price: disappointment, then outrage and frustration that the world he chose to live in, England especially, did not match his childhood dream of it. He was no longer "American," yet he remained a stranger in a strange land. Recoiling from his disappointment, he entered that phase of his career when "Form," the "figure in the carpet," became his great obsession. He emerged "as an impassioned geometer—or shall we say," Brooks wrote, "some vast arachnid of art, pouncing upon the tiny air-blown particle and wrapping it round and round." Other things passed into his style, the famous difficult style of his later manner—"the evasiveness, the hesitancy, the scrupulosity of an habitually embarrassed man":

> The caution, the ceremoniousness, the baffled curiosity, the nervousness and constant self-communion, the fear of committing himself—these traits of the self-conscious guest in the house where he had never been at home had fashioned with time the texture of his personality. They had infected the creatures of his fancy, they had fixed the character of his imaginative world; and behind

his novels, these formidable projections of a geometrical intellect, were to be discerned now the confused reveries of an invalid child. For in his prolonged association with people who had merely glimmered for him, in the constant abrogation of his moral judgment, in these years of an enchanted exile in a museum-world—for what else had England ever been for him?—Henry James had reverted to a kind of childhood. (131-32)

Brooks clinched his argument with supporting judgments from Ezra Pound and from the English critic, J. Middleton Murry, who had said that James's tragedy lay in his yearning "after the fulness of European life which he could not join again, and [so] had to satisfy his impulse of asceticism in the impassioned formalism of an art without content."

The "invalid child" Brooks had spoken of was "a Puritan child, and this child had been shocked, perpetually shocked." A Puritan inheritance—for James, a cultural inheritance at best, as for most Americans—was again held responsible by Brooks for an American artist's failure. He had pronounced this judgment quietly, however, since it was the more subtle operation of Puritanism in the Highbrow reaches of the imagination where it controlled the American's superstitious evaluation of Europe and art. From *The Wine of the Puritans* to *The Pilgrimage of Henry James* is very nearly a full circle in Brooks's work.

V *The Continuing Debate*

The publication of *The Pilgrimage of Henry James* did not start a controversy, as *The Ordeal of Mark Twain* had done, so much as it provided one of the heavier barrages in a debate already well under way over the twin issues of expatriatism and estheticism. Reviewers did divide over Brooks's critical estimate of James the novelist, though in large measure it was a predictable division that had already existed between those readers preferring James's early novels and those preferring his later, "difficult" books. Insofar as that division still prevails, though current critical estimates settle more and more upon James's later phase as his "major phase," Brooks's study remains an important defense of the superiority of James's earlier fiction as literature.

Reviewers generally greeted Brooks's study as his best book from the point of view of "literary form," but some, like Edmund Wilson, took issue with his method as one leading to misrepresentation. Edna Kenton, an authority on James, declared that Brooks's practice of "catching up a phrase here, another, there, consummating the union by a few connubial dots, with no marriage licenses, birth records, or divorce papers offered by way of footnotes and good faith, has been the method employed to the *nth* degree of polygamy in the indirect rewriting process."[13] Edmund Wilson became kinder in later judgments passed on subsequent works in which Brooks employed a similar method because he appreciated more the total effect. But Edna Kenton's strong reservation on the reliability of Brooks's scholarship became and has remained a standard objection to Brooks's later works.

Other critics, however, saw *The Pilgrimage of Henry James* as an important document in what Waldo Frank called "the classic debate" of American culture over the question of whether the American artist should stay at home. These critics used their reviews to cast their own ballots in the dispute. Brooks had his supporters in men like Frank, Newton Arvin, and the novelist of the older generation, Henry B. Fuller. Fuller reviewed the book for the *New York Times Book Review,* declaring it would endure "as a monument to one passing phase of our national development," and then, in a longer essay in the same *Book Review* a month later, on May 3, 1925, he stated that "The past ten years have not increased the credit of Europe in American eyes—least of all in those of the younger generation. . . . [Now] we can tell the expatriates of Paris, with more confidence than before, that they would do well to back-trail home and draw sustenance from their native soil and air."

Fuller may have spoken the sentiments of some of the younger generation on the expatriate issue—though, for many, it took a world-wide depression and a national crisis to send them "back-trailing"—but on the question of their pursuit of art, most of them expressed impatience with Brooks. Typically, their disfavor took the form of dismissing Brooks as a mere "sociological" critic who seemed no longer to speak to them about literature. In *Aesthete, 1925,* for instance, the one and only number of a "little magazine," a serious piece of buffoonery was thrown together one night by young men like Allen Tate, Malcolm Cowley, Kenneth Burke, Matthew Josephson, Hart Crane, and some others; and they submitted a mock grading list of America's critics which awarded Brooks "for the finding of sociological evidence,

98%. For his use of it as literary criticism, 0." The magazine as a whole was a reply to Ernest Boyd's satire of the younger writers in an article entitled "Aesthete: Model 1924" in the opening number of Mencken's *American Mercury*.

Edmund Wilson, reviewing *The Pilgrimage* for the *New Republic*, found that it was "inevitable" that Brooks's new book would raise again the "commonplace" observation that Brooks was "a social historian rather than a literary critic," and Wilson's review found Brooks incapable of recognizing the real nature of James's art. A year before, also in the *New Republic* (April 30, 1924), Wilson had voiced the same impatience with Brooks's "aesthetic sensibility" in an amusing but penetrating "imaginary dialogue" between "Mr. F. Scott Fitzgerald and Mr. Van Wyck Brooks."

There was considerable irony in Wilson's tossing the same accusation at Brooks that Brooks had earlier thrown at the older critics for their esthetic insensibility to the contemporary scene. But the final irony, after this imaginary dialogue between Fitzgerald and Brooks, lies in the actual letter Fitzgerald wrote to Brooks from Paris in June, 1925, announcing his "thrill" at the receipt of a copy of *The Pilgrimage of Henry James*. Fitzgerald thought it "above either [Wilson's] carping or [Gilbert] Seldes' tag on it," and that it was obviously of particular interest to him and his expatriate friends. Everybody over there, including Hemingway, had read it.

Whatever the carpings of the critics, whatever the shortcomings in Brooks's method, he had dramatized the complex fate of being an American in a way other artists imagined it. In April, 1925, the same month *The Pilgrimage* appeared, Fitzgerald's novel, *The Great Gatsby,* was published. It also dealt with the complex fate of an American, Jay Gatsby, whose tragedy was largely the result of his springing "from his Platonic conception of himself," from a superstitious valuation he had made, not of Europe alone, though that too figured in his makeup, but of "a vast, vulgar and meretricious beauty." Brooks was more in tune with the artist's vision of America than some of his critics credited him with being.

In the years after writing *The Pilgrimage of Henry James* Brooks modified his judgment of James hardly at all; he conceded even less to his critics than he had on his Twain book. In *Days of the Phoenix* he admitted that the "more or less" psychoanalytic method of both these books was "bound to result in distortion" by reducing each personality to a type, yet he reiterated that in each instance it was the *type* he was after and that "the case of James was really a symbol." He even confessed, "I had been quarreling with myself when I appeared to be quarreling with Henry James," but he persisted in that quarrel whenever he referred to James. Except in Brooks's biography of William Dean Howells (1959), in which James figures prominently, and in *The Dream of Arcadia* (1958), Brooks's later account of expatriate writers and artists in Italy in which the *early* James is dwelt on at some length, Brooks did not return to any sustained study of James as he did with Mark Twain.

But James is omnipresent and made to serve throughout the volumes of Brooks's *Makers and Finders* (1936-1952). He alluded to James as illustrative of "the tradition of deracination," of the "worldlier arts," and of "over-intelligent, fragile, cautious and doubtful" artists who supplanted the earlier "free, ingenuous" forms and minds that had sprung "from the soil." In his chapter on James in England, in *New England: Indian Summer*, Brooks lifted whole passages from *The Pilgrimage of Henry James*, repeating the identical language, for instance, of his charge against the later James as "some vast arachnid of art." Or more subtly, Brooks defended his thesis in a footnote, printing the corroborating judgment of a contemporary of James, after alluding in the text to "those [American writers abroad] who lost in England their feeling for the character of the people at home." Or again, though writing of Edith Wharton, he spoke of her failure "to capture the right note that Henry James had captured in so many of the American characters in his earlier books—the note that James himself had lost, the note that he had wished to lose. . . ." While thus defending his James thesis in little asides, Brooks also used James in his continuing offensive against a criticism that elevated form over content, made a cult of difficulty, and presented the later James as a kind of high priest of craftsmanship.

Jamesian himself in so many ways, in his view of his own past, in his imaginative grasp of the literary life, and in his presentation of it, Brooks paradoxically has appeared consistently in opposition to what James stands for in another of his symbolic roles as "the Master."

CHAPTER 6

The Precipitant: Emerson

THE *Dial* award for 1924 was given to Brooks "for the promise in the man," rather than for any particular work. It recognized his achievement since *America's Coming-of-Age* and gave him the leisure (with its two thousand dollar stipend) to complete *The Pilgrimage of Henry James* which eminently rounded out that achievement. In the year of its publication, 1925, his position as first among American critics was unrivaled, despite signs of growing disaffection in some of the young writers. But even the rebellious nearly always added words of praise and respect for his role as critic, whatever shortcomings they found in his recent work. *Broom,* a fiery little magazine of young esthetes and expatriates, published an attack on the *Dial* award, for instance, but explicitly disclaimed any intention to attack Brooks, "a critic of integrity." Malcolm Cowley privately assured Brooks that it was the award itself they challenged ("which by going to writers of different purposes and levels of ability has lost all its meaning") and that it was he who had chosen the word "integrity" because "it is the rarest quality in American letters."[1]

After receiving the *Dial* award Brooks was very much in demand. Scofield Thayer, one of the owners of the *Dial,* approached him in 1925 to offer him the post of editor. Later, Michael Gold asked Brooks to be editor of *New Masses.* Even Stuart Sherman, who in 1925 had become editor of *Herald-Tribune Books,* wanted Brooks's assistance, wishing "mightily you could find your way to write for us with some regularity, or even occasionally [for] you have the tone and point of view which I should like to see extended through our review."[2]

Leadership, in short, was conceded him from nearly every point on the spectrum of the American literary scene in the 1920's, from young radical "esthetes" and "expatriates," and the higher-toned, literary and arty set associated with the *Dial,* through those with wider-aiming minds like the writers for the *Herald-Tribune,* to those on the far left of political radicalism, a small though vigorously articulate group in the 1920's. Whatever their differences with one another, they found focused in Brooks their common zeal for a reinvigorated art and life in America.

The year 1925 was one of personal triumph for Brooks, and also a year of fulfillment in American letters. The two high notes coming together were not altogether a coincidence. Despite the negativism of much of his writing since the war, perhaps because of it, Brooks had carried over in the 1920's something of the "crusading spirit of the 1910's," as William Wasserstrom has noted. With Bourne gone, Brooks was the acknowledged spokesman of malcontentedness in the interests of a "higher organized life." The criticisms of the acquisitive life, of Puritanism, of the "village virus," and of the damning effects of all these upon the life of art were no longer the monopoly of a few literary radicals following Brooks's lead but commonplaces of the day.

Yet at the very moment of public triumph, Brooks struggled with a deepening private gloom. He refused every invitation tendered him to assert his leadership over a wider audience. He was not temperamentally suited for the task of editing a magazine, and the weekly deadline for the *Freeman* had taxed his energies at the expense of his larger ventures. *The Pilgrimage of Henry James* had proceeded in agonizingly slow fashion until the *Dial* award gave him the free time he needed to complete it. He had other plans, had already commenced his next work, and he wanted nothing to interfere. But the logic which compelled him to turn aside offers of public positions ran contrary to his commitment as a critic. He smarted under the criticism that he was insensitive to contemporary letters, yet increasingly he was drawn to the American past. Rereading Emerson, he shared with Lewis Mumford, who was writing *The Golden Day* (1926), the excitement of rediscovery, but by the same token he experienced doubts about his earlier reading of the Emersonian period and became more and more uncertain about the whole course and tone which his work had assumed as a consequence. These contradictions and uncertainties were difficult to resolve. The two pressures from within and without contributed to a serious nervous collapse.

For nearly six years, 1925 to 1931, Brooks withdrew from the world of letters, virtually from the world of men, and sank deeply into the sickness of a mind possessed "with a fantasy of suicide." Four years he spent in "houses of the dead, or . . . the wounded, or the about-to-be-reborn, at Stockbridge, at Katonah, at White Plains and in England." It was a long "season in hell."[3] But with the loyalty of friends, the patient care of his wife, the wise counsel of students of the psyche—Jung himself, among others— he struggled through his darkness and returned, convinced that his best years still lay ahead of him. He resumed writing almost at once, and early in 1932 he published *The Life of Emerson.*

With this book he seemed, both at the time of its appearance and in retrospect, to have moved to a new phase in his criticism. Edmund Wilson, reviewing Brooks's work up to 1940, spoke of it as falling into "two distinct divisions, with the break just before his volume on Emerson." The earlier Brooks he characterized as "somber and despairing," while the Brooks of the new phase "seemed now to be *too much* pleased with everybody; there was no longer any tension of conflict." Bernard De Voto, one of Brooks's most severe critics, who pursued him in fact as if conducting a personal vendetta, wrote in *The Literary Fallacy* that there was in Brooks's later works "a change of phase . . . radically different from the earlier ones in intention, mood, and temper." The later books were, he said, "frequently at odds with the earlier books, frequently contradict them, and come to an exact reversal of judgment."[4]

There can be no dispute about the difference in Brooks's work of the 1930's and beyond, especially the five volumes of his history of the writer in America, *Makers and Finders.* That these volumes in particular differ in "intention, mood and temper" from his prior writing is at once evident. But there is need for qualification on how much the change constituted a reversal of his critical point of view. The easy inference from Wilson's remark that Brooks had moved from discriminate rejection to indiscriminate approval requires a closer examination, as does the suspicion that this development (if accurately described) is necessarily linked to Brooks's successful recovery after his years of illness. The now public knowledge of those critical years has added greater weight to criticism that has disparaged Brooks's judgments as wholly subjective.

Such disparagement, in fact, runs through much of the criticism of Brooks's writing, even before his illness. Sherwood Anderson had wondered if some private malaise did not inhibit Brooks in his appreciation and understanding of Mark Twain, for instance; and Paul Rosenfeld had voiced a similar guess in his early essay on Brooks in the *Port of New York* (1924). Others, like Bernard Smith, trying to account for what seemed to him Brooks's decline in the 1930's, declared that it was "apparently fatal" to search inward "for either origins or solutions of social and cultural phenomena," and he found Brooks's attitude "downright unhealthy for a social critic who is committed to collectivism." Finally, Robert Spiller in the *Literary History of the United States* used the word "pathological" when relating the "morbid psychology" of Brooks's *The Ordeal of Mark Twain* to his nervous breakdown.[5]

Some facts cast doubt on these judgments and implications. The doubt, however, is not about the connection between Brooks's breakdown and his anguish over his work, for he confessed that himself. What is questionable is the easy inference that Brooks's work divides itself into two phases because of his breakdown, and that the second phase somehow cancels out the first—as if a restored self might be said to have canceled or betrayed a self suffering from a real complaint.

The Life of Emerson is the key to the problem. Published in 1932, it is readily taken as the first production of the "new" Brooks. In fact, the writing of it was completed in 1927 before Brooks's final nervous collapse. Although he had destroyed the manuscript in a moment that presaged his breakdown, his wife had rescued it and pieced it together. Even had we not Brooks's word for this, a close examination of the "Six Episodes" from the life of Emerson which first appeared in *Emerson and Others*,[6] a book his wife saw through the press, reveals the material to have been culled from the larger manuscript later published as *The Life of Emerson*. This book, even without Brooks's word, is evidently not so much a revision of the "Episodes," as the *Literary History* claims, as an expansion of them. Three entire episodes are retained intact as chapters, and every page and paragraph of the other episodes can be found scattered through the later chapters of *The Life of Emerson* with no changes except in the transitional words that had stitched them together in the original manuscript. Moreover, the "new note" that the *Literary History* claims was struck in the final paragraph of

The Life of Emerson was anticipated in the "Episodes" a half dozen times or more, and it rang just as clearly in the final paragraph of the last episode. This paragraph is nothing more than the last vibration of the thematic chord Brooks had hit in each episode, as he did in each chapter: that Emerson learned to live as One with the Universe.

Other facts of publication that announced Brooks's return to the literary life of the 1930's should cast some doubt on the description of his second phase as a "reversal." A critic's career is the history of his books as they figure in critical debates. Brooks signaled his re-entry into the stream of American criticism not only with the "new" *Emerson* but also with the collection of his "old" *Freeman* pieces, *Sketches in Criticism* (1932), and a new edition of *The Ordeal of Mark Twain* (1933), which was "revised" only in small matters of style. In fact, coming as this volume did shortly after Bernard De Voto's *Mark Twain's America* (1932), which contained a strong attack on Brooks, the revised edition may be taken as Brooks's calculated reiteration of his point of view.

In 1934, he reissued, again with only slight revision, his *America's Coming-of-Age, Letters and Leadership,* and "The Literary Life" under one cover: *Three Essays on America.* His new preface to these essays modestly cringed at his "youthful levity," conceded that the changing times had made the attack on Puritanism a bore, and called for a revision in his attitudes on America's relationship to Europe. But he was ready to defend most of the ideas he had already expressed. Plainly, the "old" Brooks had not been entirely sloughed off by the new. What *had* changed was not so much Brooks's point of view as the critical mood in America; what was "new" in the writing he commenced in the 1930's were the method and the style he developed to extend that point of view.

Brooks's absence from the American literary scene had spanned the last intoxicating years of the Jazz Age, the Crash of 1929, and the first years of the Depression. These were crucial years to miss, for they contained the renewed debate with the humanists, the lively quarrels among the host of modernist writers of every hue of liberal persuasion, and the issues they fought over. Having missed so much, Brooks could hardly have plunged knowledgeably into the literary battles that were being fought with new words and in new forums; but he was often sought out and his name was frequently included on lists of "left-wing" writers who might be expected to contribute to this or that symposium, or to endorse this or that manifesto.

Understandably, in a literary climate marked by highly disputatious language, where strong positions were strongly stated, *The Life of Emerson* came as a pale contribution. In an atmosphere tingling with the sense of crisis, alternating between desperate resignation and the expectancy of revolution, when American civilization seemed to have closed down for repairs, if not complete remodeling, the portrait Brooks gave Americans to contemplate had a puzzling irrelevancy about it. Charming, beautifully written—"a prose poem," as more than one reviewer called it—Brooks's biography, unlike his earlier books, failed to meet any evident contemporary issues. He had not shown, said one reviewer, "what Emerson can offer, in these tumultous [*sic*] times. . . ."[7]

Even had the book appeared in less tumultuous times, however, its style and method would have rendered it a curiously detached experience for the reader, then as now. Reading the book was like reading an old romance, for Brooks extended the experiment of his book on Henry James to the point that he virtually effaced his own narrative voice because he wished to invoke the very presence of Emerson himself. Ironically, so felicitous was the amalgam that the result was like a "strange fine ventriloquism," of an "attenuated voice coming from a great distance"— the words Brooks had used in "Our Poets" *a propos* of Emerson's style. When Emerson meets Hawthorne, who reminded Emerson of the "vast Cimmerian universe that lay outside his own solar track," Brooks writes:

(Not for you, Emerson, not for you to enter!—you whose sun traversed the remotest sky. A God, a God your severance ruled. Did he fear you a little, perhaps, you whose iron orbit no lesser soul could resist? Had not Ellery Channing's gait, air, voice, the turning of his eyebrow, his very thoughts come to resemble yours? Had Henry been able to resist you? His manners, the tones of his voice, his modes of expression had unconsciously followed yours for many years. How many others there were who found themselves unable to withstand your power! One could almost foresee the day when Concord would be populated with little Emersons. Wise Hawthorne, to keep you at a distance!—for who knew better than you that genius can be fatal to genius? He was friendly enough with Henry, went botanizing with him, hunting for In-

dian relics, paddling up the river: he had bought Henry's boat,
the boat of the famous "Week"—too sad for Henry to keep, now
that his brother was dead. He went fishing with Ellery, camped
with him, talked with him, laughed with him. But when you
appeared the clouds rolled over the face of the moon.)

How inviting, too, the Manse had become, with Sophia's magi-
cal touch! Emerson would never have known it, when he dropped
in of an evening. . . . What a change from the days when he
wrote his first little book there! . . .

He stole in softly. He found them there, so happy, in the midst
of all this freshness, in the beams of the great star that hung
from the ceiling, Sophia with her sewing, Hawthorne reading
aloud. Shakespeare? No, Spenser, this time: the tales of Gloriana
and the Knights. (The paradisal forest rose before him, and the
wild hills of Ireland, the fairies, dwarfs and giants, the struggle
of the soul, the shapes of evil.) Hawthorne's poet—lovelier than
a butterfly's wing. Hawthorne was fresh, too, fresh as the night-
blooming cereus. By what sorcery had he kept this dew of
youth? (187-89)

The lyrical mood, not easily sustained in prose, made for
monotony. As it was neither the tale of an ordeal nor that of a
pilgrimage, the book lacked the dramatic structure of the earlier
studies; instead, it moved in cycles from episode to episode. The
thesis that here was an American writer whose life was fully lived,
fully realized, and not compromised by his inner self was neither
explored nor argued; it was simply presented. For the fact is
that the fully lived life may be experienced, may be witnessed,
but not convincingly demonstrated.

The book failed, moreover, in its intended role as the synthesis
of the antithetical cases presented by Mark Twain and Henry
James. The first two books had addressed themselves to the
achievement of each writer as a writer. *The Life of Emerson* was
the story of a man thinking, talking, and living in society—but
not of a man writing, of an artist giving shape and form to his
thoughts and experience. The result was partly a consequence of
Brooks's method; for Emerson thinking aloud in his Journals,
talking to others through his letters, or quoting from his essays
gave little opportunity to see or measure his achievement in his
art, however these other activities might bear on the man himself. In short, the synthesis showed not the successfully realized
artist but the man. Though appropriate for a spiritual biography,
this emphasis was nevertheless not consistent with the direction

of the first two books, and *The Life of Emerson* did not achieve the neat Hegelian trilogy that Brooks had intended.

There remains the question of whether *The Life of Emerson* marks a reversal of or even a break from Brooks's earlier point of view. The revelation that Brooks had an American hero-writer he could admire, and that the hero was Emerson, should have surprised no one really familiar with his earlier work. On the other hand, the discovery of how close his affinity was with Emerson may have been something of a surprise to Brooks—a discovery that took on all the appearance of a reversal of position when he expressed it so rhapsodically in *The Life of Emerson*.

Clearly, Brooks had developed a point of view that had marked a rebirth in America of "the old subjective ethos of romanticism sixty years after the decline of Emersonism." Brooks's organic view of society; his assumption that great literature proceeded from great lives, from fulfilled personalities; his early quarreling with rationalism and with mechanism, and his impatience with mere technique—all these views, although they may have derived immediately from Ruskin, William Morris, Yeats, and other Europeans, had an American lineage traceable to Emerson. Nowhere is Brooks's faith in the self at one with its world clearer than in his early confessional essays, *The Soul* and *The Malady of the Ideal*. But it is also true that in his early polemical works, *The Wine of the Puritans* and *America's Coming-of-Age*, an ambiguous attitude toward Emerson prevailed, the product of youthful ignorance in part, but also of the demands of the critical battles of the day. When Brooks started to write, Emerson had been captured by the Emersonians; and in his attack on their arid gentility Brooks necessarily struck at them through Emerson. Even Irving Babbitt, though he had some reservations, made Emerson serve the humanist cause; and it would hardly have been tactful for Brooks to endorse unequivocally an idol of the opposition.

Brooks was equivocal, however, in his attitude toward Emerson and his New England circle; and appreciation of this fact makes *The Life of Emerson* not a reversal but a resolution, not a break but an extension. In *America's Coming-of-Age* Brooks had attacked Emerson as the patron saint of a whole host of "baccalaureate ideals," but he had also declared that on the personal plane Emerson was a possession forever: "in the world of spirit" Emerson truly lived, alone of all American writers, for having given "some kind of basis to American idealism." To him, Emerson "perfectly combined the temperaments of Jonathan Edwards and Benjamin Franklin."[8] The upper and lower levels of the American mind had become fused in Emerson. And, finally, Brooks had believed that "in days to come" Emerson would "sound and shine over a better world." *The Life of Emerson* had attempted to hasten that day.

CHAPTER 7

Creating a Usable Past

I *Makers and Finders*

WHEN Brooks wrote that "A people is like a ciphered parchment which has to be held up to the fire before its hidden significances come out" in *America's Coming-of-Age,* he could with some truth add that no serious attempt had yet been made "to bring about the necessary contraposition of forces, to divine them, to detach them, to throw them into relief," to create a "resisting background" in the vague element of American life. And this was the task he set for himself when he returned to his writing in 1932. For the next twenty years he labored to discover the "thousand potential currents and cross-currents" in American life—to create them, "like works of art"; to create "a usable past." The result was *Makers and Finders: A History of the Writer in America, 1800-1915,* in five volumes. The work was Brooks's *magnum opus,* the logical end toward which his whole career had pointed. It must be counted among the major achievements in American creative scholarship; unique in its attempt, aim, and purpose, it was singularly Brooks's in its final accomplishment.

These are, however, the volumes over which Brooks's critics divide in their estimate of his career. These books mark the swing in his reputation from that of a leader of literary radicalism to that of spokesman for literary conservatism—a leader of the "Middlebrow Counter Revolution."[1] Just as the *Dial* award in 1924 had singled him out for his first role, so the Pulitzer Prize in 1936—awarded for *The Flowering of New England,* the first volume of the series to be written—seemed to stamp him in his latter role and to mark his capture by a "middlebrow" audience. But the hasty conclusion that Brooks had effected a turnabout needs to be checked, both by an examination of the nature of his *Makers and Finders* and by an understanding of the changing critical moods which greeted each of the volumes as they appeared over a sixteen-year span: *The Flowering of New England* (1936); *New England: Indian Summer* (1942); *The World of Washington Irving* (1944); *The Times of Melville and Whitman* (1947); and *The Confident Years: 1885-1915* (1952). Although Brooks himself recommended a different order of reading, the purpose and method behind the whole are more clearly seen if one is aware first of the way Brooks discovered his subject.

The method of each volume is integral with theme and purpose: to uncover and make available the actual presence of the American past, the presence of a tradition among American writers. Not concerned so much with defining that tradition, Brooks simply presented it to demonstrate its existence. That "well-known abstraction, the American writer," Brooks found in all his particular varieties. Each writer formed part of a continuum of experience with America that added up to Brooks's story: the history of the writer as a member of a kind of guild —a class that was part of, yet distinct from, the history of other Americans. Writers were distinguished from other Americans as men thinking, feeling, and writing about their thoughts and sensations. They were men who engaged their personalities with that of America: men who found themselves in a style that contributed to the making of a democratic style of letters.

The technique Brooks used to uncover this continuum was that of the narrator of a romance. Brooks created the settings— the Boston of Gilbert Stuart, Dr. Holmes's Boston, Philadelphia in 1880, Washington Irving's New York, New York in the 1880's —each filled out with the details that had been vivid to the people who roamed through them. He introduced his characters as they emerged from worlds of their own making into the larger world of their fellows. Between them, Brooks traced a detailed pattern of action and reaction—between writers; between them and the places and events they moved through or were moved by; between them and their essays, their histories, their novels, poems, plays, letters, journals, and memoirs, and he employed nearly every scrap of the published record of the writer's life.

The connections were what fascinated Brooks, and he discovered them in his reading and in the rigorous daily routine of saturation in the words and worlds of the men and women he wrote about. At the same time he developed his own skill at showing them: his sentences, with quick deft touches or lengthy parentheses, grew weighty and dense with cross references and echoes. His paragraphs evoked scenes furnished with authentic details gleaned from a dozen different sources. To retrace Brooks's steps in the gathering of the details that go to form any one of his paragraphs is no small piece of research, and the effort reveals not only his painstaking reading but the artistry and cunning with which he arranged what he found into a meaningful pattern.

The design is also revealed in the way some of the same details are likely to occur in a later chapter or in a later volume. Changed somewhat by time or by appearing in a different place, his details no less than his characters become living parts of a community. What had first served to round out a particular personality, setting him in his own time and place as he then and there looked, reappears to enrich his significance, to extend that personality through time and across space into that realm called Tradition. Organically ordered, *Makers and Finders* aimed, at least, to make an American tradition solid and alive and present rather than, as Brooks had experienced it as a young man, abstract, dead, and past.

Starting from the connection he had most recently rediscovered between himself and Emerson, Brooks began with that part of the American cultural past that most clearly possessed homogeneity. Then a race of writers in close neighborly communion had articulated a national purpose: the shared conviction among Americans that they were building a civilization. *The Flowering of New England* remains the best of the five volumes precisely for that reason, and each of the succeeding volumes gives an answer to the question implicit on every page of the first: if Americans once had this organic relationship with one another, with their land, with their sense of purpose and destiny, and if they once had transcended the barriers of province and had once discoursed in universals, in what way did a literary heritage and culture develop? The question is really no different in substance from the question Brooks had raised time and time again earlier in his career, only the method is now that of synthesis rather than of analysis.

The Flowering of New England is the story of the emergence of an organic community of writers and artists. Brooks began his tale quietly, concentrating on the actual community, the Boston scene in the years following the Peace of Ghent; on Harvard College in 1815; and on the coastal scene up and down from there and the hinterland beyond. Representatives of the Revolutionary generation and their sons, sharing in associations and recollections, were still around. John Adams and his son John Quincy Adams, both scholar-statesmen, set a tone of high national purpose. A warm, chivalrous Tory strain lingered too, not otherworldly, but presenting a placid, genial surface, a "magnificent style" of living. Underneath, Boston tingled with new ambitions. Younger men, quixotic souls, thought of going to sea. "In every corner of this New England country . . . a fresh, a more vigorous spirit was plainly astir."

Touching on the evidence from hundreds of sources, Brooks built upon this note of expectation, and then introduced the individual talents who contributed to the community's fulfillment: George Ticknor, the social and intellectual figure; Daniel Webster, the political figure; and William Ellery Channing, the religious figure—each of them preparing the ground for literature by their "harrowing of the ground for life." The literary minds stirred in Boston, hundreds issued a summons for a literature that was really American, and then Brooks settled on those who had answered, the historians: Jared Sparks, George Bancroft, William Prescott, and still later the younger John Lothrop Motley. Brooks's treatment of each was full and discriminating, comparing their works to those from across the sea.

Then, effecting a transition and at the same time establishing the connecting links that make for a community, Brooks introduced his first major New England talent, the young Henry Wadsworth Longfellow, applying for lodging at Craigie House in 1837 where Jared Sparks and Edward Everett had lived before him, and where lexicographer Dr. Joseph Worcester then lived and worked on his *American Dictionary*. In later days, Brooks confessed, Longfellow's poems would seem pale and without distinction, but during his first years in Cambridge he "spoke for the youth of all the world." Through Longfellow, the American community reached out and touched a larger one, a community of youth, of young ideas, of new beginnings. Disaffected with civilization as it was, the younger generation of 1840 protested against a world bred on commercial interests and isolation and suffering from "an excess of prudence, compromise, provincial good taste." The young men turned instead to reaffirm the senses and the soul, to read Keats and Tennyson, to be stirred by the critical ideas of Coleridge, to succumb to the style and thought of Carlyle, to listen to winds of doctrine coming from Germany. But their real prophet was already among them, a New Englander, Ralph Waldo Emerson.

With his first chapter on Emerson (a later one dealt with the more solitary Emerson, with Emerson the poet), Brooks reached the heart and center of his book. Emerson was the talent and the tradition joined, the independent talent that articulated a tradition of independence, of reliance upon the inner voice which was also the voice of the collective psyche, of Emerson's Oversoul. All the other New England eccentrics found justification in his doctrine and so joined hands in a community of eccentrics. Nathaniel Hawthorne, who "had shaped a poetic personality as valid and distinct as Emerson's," was equally an articulator for and contributor to this community, despite all his darkness and sense of doom in contrast to Emerson's philosophical optimism. Brooks's chapter on "Hawthorne in Salem," one of his most successful blendings of personality and milieu, placed this legendary figure of solitude more firmly within a living community. A succeeding chapter on the Brook Farm experiment, with considerable attention given to Bronson Alcott and Margaret Fuller, showed the community widening its reach and influence.

In this manner Brooks's form and theme became one as he alternated between discussions of the larger community—a generation, the Concord scene in the 1840's—and an individual artist—Emerson, Hawthorne, Thoreau, the older Longfellow, James Russell Lowell, Whittier, Holmes, and so on. But, nearing the end of the limits of the "flowering"—the Civil War—Brooks's note of rich fulfillment subsided; he hinted at decline, at the community's breaking-up. The chapter on "The Romantic Exiles" (various writers and artists from Hawthorne to William Wetmore Story who had gone abroad) anticipated a central difference, if not quite the cause of decline, between the years of flowering and those of Indian Summer. With Emerson leading the censure against the "tapeworm of Europe," the pre-Civil War Yankee mind had faced Europe with "serene aplomb," only mildly indulging an "idle and pathetic nostalgia for Europe." Brooks's conclusion underscored this strong sense of a native community as cause of artistic fulfillment and its disruption as a sign of artistic decline. The movement of the New England mind, he said, followed a typical Spenglerian pattern of a "culture-cycle."

There had been, first of all, "a homogeneous people, living close to the soil, intensely religious, unconscious, unexpressed in art and letters, with a strong sense of home and fatherland." One of the towns of this community—Boston, with Cambridge and Concord as suburbs—becomes one of Spengler's "culture-cities" and acts as mouthpiece for the country, giving vent to "the springtime feeling in the air." An unconscious pride manifests itself in the founding of institutions. Timid at first, "the mind begins to shape into myths and stories the dreams of the pre-urban countryside" until "a moment of equipoise" is reached, "a widespread flowering of the imagination in which the thoughts and feelings of the people, with all their faiths and hopes find expression." But then the mind gradually becomes "detached from the soil" and grows more and more self-conscious:

> Contradictions arise within it, and worldlier arts supplant the large, free, ingenuous forms through which the poetic mind has taken shape. What formerly grew from the soil begins to be planned. The Hawthornes yield to the Henry Jameses. Over-intelligent, fragile, cautious and doubtful, the soul of the culture-city loses the self-confidence and joy that have marked its early development,—it is filled with a presentiment of the end; and the culture-city itself surrenders to the world-city—Boston surrenders to New York. . . . What has once been vital becomes provincial; and the sense that one belongs to a dying race dominates and poisons the creative mind (540, Everyman ed.).

The meaning of this culture-cycle was one Brooks had long committed himself to expound, harkening back to the commitment of the young prophets of pre-World War I days. It was, said Brooks, as D. H. Lawrence had voiced it, that "men are free when they are in a living homeland, not when they are straying and breaking away . . . when they are obeying some deep, inward voice of religious belief . . . when they belong to a living, organic, believing community, active in fulfilling some unfulfilled, perhaps unrealized purpose."

New England: Indian Summer, as the title suggests, presented a literary landscape where "the sweetness of a ripe October" clung, with buds beginning to form but overshadowed still by the late, lingering leaves. Hawthorne was gone, as was Thoreau;

but some of the other figures from the *Flowering* were still around, their activities and status now symbolized in the Dante meetings around Longfellow at Craigie House, where they gave themselves over to translating and celebrating the great of the past, their own teachers and models. This order of permanence in the post-Civil War years was best seen, on the surface at least, in idyllic "Whittierland," the rural reaches between sea and mountain, or at leisurely Newport. But there were changes in this scene too, hard "secular" problems of the moment—the shifting population, abandoned farms, the factory system and newly rich, the corruption in politics—which the older personalities seemed ill-equipped to meet. "Too much of the Emersonian bred an indifference to the hard facts of American life [which] had never gone so wrong as immediately after the war."[2] The New England mind retreated into itself.

Into this scene where change battled with permanence, Brooks introduced the young William Dean Howells, an ambitious Howells prepared as poet and student to combat this retreating mentality on its own terms and to triumph over it, finally, by heeding in his fiction the Emersonian counsel to sit at the feet of the low and familiar. Howells recorded the permanence and the changes, and thus to some extent he reconciled the two, achieving a broad democratic feeling for life. Brooks wove his treatment of Howells in and out of nearly every chapter, making him function in this volume as Emerson had in the earlier one. Emersonian, but not too much so, from the West and with years of travel and residence in Europe, Howells assimilated to the New England mentality not only his background but his experience abroad. Howells served Brooks as a preserver and extender of tradition, both in his capacity as an individual artist and as a critic, friend, and editor who nurtured other individual talents. Howells managed to preserve a semblance of a living community of writers, if only through the myriad of writers and artists he met and counseled.

Except for the cohesive force of Howells, the energies of nearly every other writer Brooks introduced into this Indian Summer world suffered division. The question of "facing the new America" seemed overwhelming to most of the younger generation of the 1870's. In despair of the civilization before them, these men—like Clarence King, the younger Agassiz, Henry Adams, Henry James, or the painter James Whistler—turned either westward to meet "the reckless life" of the West with its "hardships and fever of speculation . . . ruined health and broken souls and madness," or to Europe, as in the instances of James and Whistler, there to achieve pre-eminence as "masters of technical processes" but to lose their sense of the "native character," and ultimately to lose faith in the choice they had made.

Some few avoided the fires of the West and of Europe, chose the frying-pan by settling in the East to cultivate their own talents, "and paid the full price of their courage that later times revered as noble grandsires"—men like Winslow Homer and Albert Pinkham Ryder, the architects H. H. Richardson and Louis Sullivan, "builders in the line of Emerson and Whitman" who showed "that a native integrity was better than a borrowed nobility." Howells was in this line too, much as Europe and the West had meant to him also; but he was almost the sole counterbalance in the book to the centrifugal forces of those men like Henry James and Henry Adams who were thrown back upon themselves and who lost "the inherited ties that bound them to the population."

James was, in fact, nearly as important a presence as Howells in *New England: Indian Summer.* Essentially the James of Brooks's *Pilgrimage,* he was, however, a James whose "curious Anglicism" Brooks sought to make comprehensible by setting it in the social context where it was formed. The literal, the historical, and the imaginative quests for certainty of Henry Adams (an Adams who knew what writers needed—a *school*—and knew it was out of the question for his time), filled out the dimensions of another lonely, divided figure, as did Brooks's single chapter on Emily Dickinson, a poetess who made up in "intensity" and in her "sharp perception of values" for the defeats she had known and the love she had lost.

Concluding the book with the period of the 1890's and the prewar years, Brooks artfully blended his account of the retrospective mood of the New England mind come full circle in Henry Adams, a mood shading a sense of regret and defeat into the signs of the renaissance that was to come, visible between the lines in the country pictures of Mary E. Wilkins and Sarah Orne Jewett, or in the "Emersonian gleam," dim and shrouded though it was, in the poems of E. A. Robinson. At the point of Robert Frost's return from England in 1915, Brooks's final chapter swiftly and with skillful economy brought together the harbingers of a "second march" of the Yankee mind, the tradition which could not be permitted to languish because all Americans were implicated in it.

For *The World of Washington Irving*, Brooks went back in time to a lesser culture-cycle. Covering the years 1800-1840, it preceded and overlapped the cycle of New England's flowering. It had its own pulsations, different from those of the New England cycle, with shorter intervals, swinging back and forth between rudimentary "world-cities"—Philadelphia, New York, Charleston, and back to New York again. Following the manner of the earlier books, *The World of Washington Irving* literally teemed with the presence of the writers and artists whose lives crossed and recrossed and moved from city to city, region to region, and to Europe and back again. Their works spoke a national consciousness, broad where the New England mind ran deep, "planetary" rather than universal, different in its cosmopolitanism yet concentric with and meeting at a number of points the cycle of tradition from New England.

Irving, James Fenimore Cooper, William Cullen Bryant, and Edgar Allan Poe were the dominant figures, each sharing nearly equal emphasis. Overshadowing these, however (giving the book its unity as did Emerson and Howells in the New England volumes) was the presence of Jefferson—not his actual personage so much as the lingering impact of his mind and its expansive "planetary interests" containing "principles . . . of universal meaning." In Jefferson Brooks found "the earliest crystallization of the American prophetic tradition," the tradition found in Whitman, Emerson, and in Lincoln's "mystical faith in the wisdom of the people." Virtually every writer of eminence in this period "followed the Jeffersonian line."

Virtually all followed Jefferson, that is, except for Poe. Yet, forcing the contrast—"if [Poe] had been politically minded, one might have thought of him as a type of the anti-Jeffersonian Southern reaction"—Brooks used him to underscore his own belief in the strength of the tradition flowing from Jefferson: "Nothing could have proved more clearly the toughness and reality of the American tradition than the patent fact that Poe *was* outside it." In other respects, Brooks gave Poe just and discriminating analysis as "a literary genius that had had no parallel as yet on the American scene." He, moreover, was "supremely artistic" and "a conscious master of his methods as well as his effects."

As a critic, he wrote about literature as an art "when this was the one thing necessary." It was not Poe, however, but the others who constituted the community, who were closely connected with public life, and who shared "the buoyant confidence of the expanding nation, with its Jeffersonian freight of morning dreams . . . ."

A typical narrative flourish—"In and about New York, meanwhile, two writers of genius were coming of age, Walt Whitman . . . and Herman Melville"—and a final allusion to the New Englanders who "on their home-ground were already overshading the writers of all other regions" brought this cycle to a close and anticipated the emergence of yet another, growing out of and drawing upon both the New England and Jeffersonian cycles. *The Times of Melville and Whitman* commenced in chronology and setting where *The World of Washington Irving* left off— New York in the 1840's—and extended into the 1880's, thus overlapping each of the preceding volumes.

This volume too had its own peculiar rhythm that defined still another distinct movement in the culture-cycle. Though it shared characteristics with each of the others, it moved less between cities, or swung out from a single culture-city, but more between regions, suggesting, through Melville, Whitman, and Mark Twain, the making of a universal discourse, yet one still different from that achieved by the New Englanders. The title might more accurately have included Mark Twain who shares equal attention with Whitman and Melville. Unlike the earlier volumes, this one had no single unifying talent or mind to give coherence to this impulse of tradition. A pattern of unity was provided instead by a triangle of talents, with Whitman at its apex and Melville and Twain poised at connecting but opposite vertices. The area between them, "the West," was filled with the dreams of Jefferson, the prophetic utterances of Emerson, and the near mystical person of Lincoln—a West that was a region of the American mind, that contained the essential American tradition created by these talents.

Finally, in the last volume of the series, *The Confident Years, 1885-1915,* Brooks took up the cycle whose definitive rhythms had pushed his own generation into rebellion and renewal. Appropriately, Brooks commenced his tale with the arrival of James Huneker in New York City in the year of his own birth, 1886. Huneker, the critic who was to bring a new note of cosmopolitanism into American letters, was one of the immediate ancestors behind the "inter-racial" and "transnational" emphases of Mencken, Bourne, Pound, and others of Brooks's generation. Although Brooks gave due importance to the veneer of "confidence" in the years before World War I—symbolized for Brooks in the figure of Theodore Roosevelt—his book was chiefly about the rebels who had become disenchanted with that age's complacency and who had hurled vehement challenges at it for the failures to maintain the progress of the American dream. For most of them—from Stephen Crane, Frank Norris, Ambrose Bierce, Jack London, and Theodore Dreiser, in the 1890's and turn of the century, to Eugene O'Neill whose appearance at the end of the book promised a full resurgence—"the gap had widened between reality and the idea." They were denunciatory in proportion to their steadfastness to "the idea," and thus they had "continued to express the traditional American faith."

Some few writers did not, of course. Some were opposed to the main current of contemporary feeling. Others, moreover, reacted from outside the American tradition, like Paul Elmer More, whom Brooks scourged as severely as he had in earlier days. To Mencken he gave much credit for delivering a death blow to colonialism and for contributing to "the nationalizing of American letters," but Mencken too was fundamentally antagonistic to the mainstream of the American past. While rightly attacking efforts like Stuart Sherman's to restore the Anglo-Saxon tradition, Mencken had failed to see, because he had no "inherited knowledge" of the American past, that it was not the restoration of that past but its *recognition*—"the re-establishing of a living relation between the future and the past"—that was relevant and desirable. T. S. Eliot, although he had "reaffirmed the transcendent importance of tradition" at a moment when many young writers deliberately sought "to turn themselves into barbarians," had brought to a head this tendency to reverse the American tradition; he had, in fact, been actively hostile to it.

But others in the younger generation of 1915—the "last of the younger generations that had its roots in the nineteenth century" —though also rebels conscious of the country's faults, "of the Spoon Rivers and the Tilbury Towns, the Zeniths and Winesburgs and Gopher Prairies," and repelled by the "debris of a hasty civilization" with its rampant Philistinism and vulgarity, were nonetheless aware "of the sanative mind-stirring forces that were coming to birth" in America. They shared the perennial faith in the American future, and they were the real makers and finders of the American tradition.

Among them, of course, was Brooks himself, though kept anonymous, "a younger writer" who announced that "America was at last 'coming of age.'" But chiefly, there was Randolph Bourne, to whom Brooks assigned the center among the young intellectuals of faith—the writers who believed that art could help men to shape and adorn civilization. These, rather than the nay-sayers, were the preserving talents and the extenders of "the main body of American tradition."

Makers and Finders has seemed to some readers like a novel, a novel of saturation, with each of its parts alive in each of its other parts. But in its total cumulative thrust, it is even more nearly a romance. It has more to do with the clouds overhead— with those abstractions "the American writer" and "American literary culture"—than with the actual soil of American literature: its language, images, forms, and themes. As a romance, it is the story of Brooks's own experience with a legend prolonging itself. It is a fable, perhaps, as some critics have implied—but a fable whose density of fact and skillful narration make it ring true.

II   *The Form of Tradition*

Brooks's critics have addressed themselves to questioning the nature and extent of the truth of his history, and to assessing his changing role as a critic in the writing of it. Brooks invited some of this criticism when he first announced that his subject in *The Flowering of New England* was "the New England mind" and that it was the first of a series of volumes to sketch "the literary history of the United States." His second book he also called part of "the history of American literature," and his third again was one of a series on "the literary history of the United States." Not until *The Times of Melville and Whitman* did he refer to his work as "the history of the literary life in America," but the final label, *A History of the Writer in America*, was not added to the whole until the final volume. Consequently, as the early volumes appeared, most of his critics tried to define what he had done by taking issue with him for what he had not done.

It was neither "social or intellectual history in any strict sense," nor even "formal literary history" to F. O. Matthiessen, who complained in a *New York Times* book review (October 1, 1944) that Brooks did not really place works in their milieu; that he was little concerned with genres; and, since he was "almost wholly indifferent to technical analysis," that he raised few issues about structure or form. The "image of our past" seemed to Edmund Wilson "a little too even and cheerful." He missed the "stress of the period" of Melville and Whitman and felt that Brooks's truth was not the whole truth.[3]

Bernard De Voto, looking only at the first two New England volumes, objected that all the agony, grief, despair, and frustration in the lives of the writers Brooks wrote about had been omitted, or colored over by the pastel strokes of his prose. Under Brooks's treatment, De Voto complained, the New England writers were "forever threatening to degenerate into esthetes." He found little "intensity" in them, "except the intensity of writers mastering a literary medium . . . little struggle in them except the struggle of writers trying to give idea a garment of words . . . little violence or even vehemence of thought, and hardly any of feeling." The cause De Voto attributed to the one thread of continuity he would concede between the work of Brooks's first period and his mature work: "an indifference to the common experience of mankind," which De Voto related to "the literary fallacy." "It is a criticism of books, out of books, by the sole means of books, to the sole end of books," doomed to fail as both history and criticism because it assumed that culture could be appraised by purely literary criteria.[4]

But, generally, criticism of this kind concentrated the blame on Brooks's narrative method. "It is a method," Edmund Wilson said of *The Flowering of New England,* "which involves what amounts to an abdication of the critic."[5] Lionel Trilling, with the completed series before him, extended this judgment to Brooks's career and spoke of *Makers and Finders* as marking Brooks's "abdication of his leadership of the modern movement." For Trilling, Brooks's method, though praiseworthy in its intention, evoked a memory of America's cultural past which "never seems to be anything but an enchanting dream because ideas and the conflict of ideas play little or no part in it." This characteristic seemed ironic to Trilling when viewed against Brooks's early work which had pleaded for a national existence wherein "ideas should be related to the actual life of a people."[6]

Trilling's judgment, a mixture of praise for Brooks's intention and a sad shaking of the head over the result, is representative of the critical response to Brooks's later work that now passes as the consensus. Brooks's aim was a noble one, so the judgment goes; but with *Makers and Finders,* and thereafter, his powers as a critic declined. To some extent this judgment is the unfortunate consequence of reviewers' repeating themselves and one another until criticism addressed in the first place to individual volumes of Brooks's series has been taken as applicable to the whole of *Makers and Finders.* That is to say—to risk repeating what has already been suggested and anticipating the next chapter—Brooks's volumes appeared, one by one, during a time of changing literary fashions, when criticism, analytical criticism in particular, was in the ascendent and literary history not only declined in prestige but became suspect as an instrument for promoting extremes of nationalism. Ironically, this fact in turn has amounted to a neglect of Brooks's intention, not as he declared it to be, which has often been pounced upon all too literally, but as it lies revealed in the final form and shape of the whole.

It is ironic that criticism which has charged Brooks with insensitivity or indifference to matters of form and style should appear so indifferent to the form of his completed *Makers and Finders.* Favorable reviewers, like Lewis Mumford, have found Brooks's work almost flawless if read on its own terms; and others have reached for words like "pageant" and "tapestry" to describe the effect of his narrative technique in individual volumes. Such words, however, though they may suggest the manner of narration, connote static landscape artistry and do not do full justice to the resulting shape. Lewis Mumford's metaphor, likening the narrative flow to "the mighty Hudson, hardly changing its direction, never altering the rate of flow, carrying the silt, the pebbles, and the boulders at about the same rate and about the same level,"[7] is more apt. Even this figure, however, repeating as it does Edmund Wilson's objection that Brooks failed to discriminate between major and minor writers, does not convey the alterations in tone and tempo—as between discussion of an individual writer and that of his setting in time and space—that are present in each volume, nor the cyclical rhythm in the series as a whole. The movement courses a time-stream from 1800 and into the present, yet not solely in the single linear direction that Mumford's metaphor implies.

The final order Brooks gave to the series was a concession to chronology, but his final vision of the shape of tradition and the way it grew was not radically different from the way he discovered it. That is to say, the tradition was still present as organic, as a breathing in and out and a movement back and forth. Looked at in this ordering of the volumes, it would appear that Brooks had finally conceived of literary tradition in America as the result of action and interaction between cultural cycles of different regions and different times, with each cycle in turn defined by a similar kind of drama among the personalities each contained.

Thus, *Makers and Finders* began with the first mild notes of nationalism in 1800 that were sounded in Philadelphia, New York, New England, the South, and the West and given force and meaning by Jefferson, Irving, Cooper, Bryant, and Poe (*The World of Washington Irving*). Before this cycle completed itself (by the 1840's), *The Flowering of New England* recorded the beginnings of a second nationalistic impulse with the Peace of Ghent in 1815, and showed its derivation and growth in a region of mind with cosmopolitan and even cosmic pretensions—New England. Boston, and Harvard with its amateur scholars—Ticknor, Bancroft, Prescott, then Longfellow, Lowell, Hawthorne, Holmes, Whittier, Emerson and Thoreau—defined this cycle by their collective personalities and, carrying something of the first cycle with them, created what Brooks thereafter judged as the main stalk of America's literary tradition. The third volume, *The Times of Melville and Whitman,* took shape partly from the impact between the first two, derived strength from Washington Irving's New York of the 1840's and from Melville's experience in the Berkshires, but assumed its own peculiar outline and force from the newer nationalism of Whitman, Lincoln, the Far West and Mark Twain, and from the South of Jefferson and Poe that had suffered Civil War and defeat, the South of Sidney Lanier.

New England: Indian Summer began quietly, with the arrival in post-Civil War Boston of William Dean Howells, out of Ohio by way of Venice; but from the pressures of figures like Howells, James, Henry Adams, and Emily Dickinson, it gathered its own momentum, merged with the other cycles somewhat, and by its end was gathering renewed energy from the potential that vibrated in *The Flowering of New England* and promised another flowering, another resurgence. Volume V, *The Confident Years,* started where the third left off, at a transitional moment in the 1880's; gathered impetus from each preceding volume as it swept over the regions again and into the new cosmopolitan centers, the San Francisco of Frank Norris and Jack London, Chicago in the 1890's, uptown New York and Stephen Crane's East Side, to Lafcadio Hearn in Japan and the Yellow Book circle in England; then in its final chapters, after Dreiser, Mencken, the younger generation of 1915 and the renascence that had been promised at the end of Volume IV, it arrived at the present.

To read *Makers and Finders* in this order, but mindful too of the order of discovery, one may observe—contrary to F. O. Matthiessen who described Brooks's method as "diffuse" involving a "casual" way of treating Time[8]—that Brooks's "intention" to create a usable past has been rendered through a remarkably sophisticated treatment of Time, which is not simply a casual or incidental frame for the narrator, but the very stuff on which the story moves and in which each writer of his story is immersed. This way of looking at tradition as alive subordinates conflict within particular cycles of pulsation in order to see the larger give and take between and across the major impulses.

It is also instructive to read in succession from volume to volume those chapters that deal with similar and recurring themes: those on the several "younger generations," on American writers abroad, or on different kinds of Bohemian impulses and a burgeoning art-consciousness. So read and so ordered, these chapters then add up to individual volumes of more conventional literary history that are devoted to tracing themes like the recurring romantic rebellion in American letters (the cultivation of individual talents), the persisting tug of Europe upon the American imagination (the cultivation of the sense of tradition), or the story of the developing self-consciousness of art and craftsmanship in the culture-cities of a democracy. *Makers and Finders* provides, in short, the materials of literary history, as Whitman said his *Leaves of Grass* offered the materials of poetry. And, like Whitman's organic poem, Brooks's work presents his materials in the organic relationships in time and space as he found them there.

The form of *Makers and Finders* does not regard the culture of a nation as a current, the way Parrington's history did; nor does it present "the form of its existence" as "struggle," "debate," or "a dialectic," as Lionel Trilling sees it. But this characteristic does not mean, as Trilling concludes, that "ideas and the conflict of ideas play little or no part in it."[9] There is no "conflict," in the sense of clash between opposites, thesis and antithesis. The form precludes that kind of clash. But there is give and take, absorption and repulsion across the cycles. And two of the controlling ideas that move across each volume, providing between them the tension in the history of the American writer, are those of "the individual talent" on the one hand and of "tradition" on the other. As Brooks's final title suggests, the American writer had both to find and to make his native talent and to discover and make his native tradition. Tension exists among the several ideas of genius and tradition which American writers created and represented in their collective careers.

For Brooks, this process and interplay between finding and making—participated in by a "great body of writers from Benjamin Franklin down to a regiment of poets, romancers, historians and thinkers"—had provided, in literature, the special character of American culture and was, in fact, "the core of America." In the concluding chapter of *The Confident Years,* where he made this summation, he defined this core as "the liberal-democratic American tradition . . . quite as much as any other an outgrowth and a strand of the great European tradition" that existed in every modern country; but it "stood for the whole nature of America and expressed its uniqueness."

CHAPTER 8

The Critic and the Critics

WHEN Brooks pointed to the "liberal-democratic American tradition" as the core of America's uniqueness, he oversimplified the actual complexity of his *Makers and Finders*. The American literary tradition in Brooks's work is not simply the liberal Jeffersonian tradition in politics and economics as Parrington made it out to be in his "literary history," *Main Currents in American Thought*. Brooks's final stated definition consequently appears to contradict the shape and form of *Makers and Finders* itself, and this contradiction is related to the way Brooks seemed to have betrayed his own early writing.

He had felt and experienced the sense of a still living American literary past that extended into the present. The success of *Makers and Finders* in fact lies in the way it imaginatively created a living, felt tradition. But when Brooks approached and entered the time stream he himself had swirled, the myth-maker in him gave way to the advocate; the creative objectivity achieved by his narrative voice yielded to the partisan tones of the critic and polemicist—and to the prophet who would have the future match and prolong his image of the growing, living past. His dilemma was that of one who would have the organic view impose on life the coherence and unity of art. Brooks's voice became a living voice among other living voices, defending himself and advocating a program. That program—an expression of faith—could appear, however, only as a kind of pseudopodium in the organic scheme of the past, connecting yet reaching out in its own singular direction.

Explanation of the disagreement between the shape of an American tradition in his work and his statement defining it need not rest alone on the dilemma implicit in Brooks's point of view, however. It may be found also in the way Brooks as critic figured in the critical debates of the 1930's and early 1940's. They were years of highly charged literary warfare, mixed and stirred in the emotional ferment over Communism, Fascism, and the war; and nothing less than the course of democratic American culture was the issue. These same years marked the appearance of vital American writing, sophisticated in form and style, and incisive in its probing of the modern temper. This writing was accompanied, moreover, by formidable criticism whose skillful and confident assessment helped secure its reputation. Politics and esthetics commanded nearly equal attention and snuggled comfortably together in the same journals, an article starting from one invariably ending up in a comment on the other. For a while, the higher organized life that Brooks and his associates had called for in the days of World War I seemed to be operating.

In the closing chapters of *The Confident Years* Brooks resumed his lifelong warfare with esthetes, expatriates, and Puritans; and in opposition to these, he reaffirmed his own Emersonian vision. "A Forward Glance," the last chapter, found him engaged once again in a dispute with the nay-sayers. In particular, he leveled his sights on T. S. Eliot, whose name Brooks employed much in the way Irving Babbitt had used Rousseau's. It was in the context of his dispute with Eliot that Brooks offered his definition of the uniqueness of America, charging Eliot and his followers with having largely ignored the Jeffersonian vision of the future. Though judicious and temperate in tone, this chapter was a restatement of Brooks's position in one of the more bitter episodes in modern American letters; consequently, it still bore the marks of polemical debate.

An echo of the fracas over "the irresponsibles" set off by Archibald MacLeish early in 1940, this chapter showed Brooks as again defending his position in that dispute and as still smarting from the countercharges that had been hurled at him. In turn, reviewers of *Makers and Finders,* especially of the volumes appearing during the renewed nationalist sentiment of the war years, could seldom avoid the temptation to revive or at least recall that quarrel. The reputation of the whole of *Makers and Finders* has consequently been colored, not alone by that particular debate, but by the full complex of the literary warfare of the 1930's which led to it.

I   *The Humanists Again*

As has been noted, Brooks himself had withdrawn from the literary scene before the opening of this quarrelsome decade. He and his followers had figured prominently, however, in the literary battle over humanism which had closed the 1920's and had set the tone for the conflicts of the 1930's.

Norman Foerster, self-appointed defender of the humanist cause, gathered his forces together in the collection of essays entitled *Humanism and America* (1930) in which he boldly challenged the whole achievement of the young modernists' writing since World War I. Foerster singled out Brooks in particular as the leader whose "controlling ideas" for this modernist movement had proven utterly inadequate, even perhaps non-existent. Other defenders, like Gorham B. Munson, made similar accusations, also aimed at Brooks as the chief offender against humanist values. In a surprisingly short time the number of replies to this first symposium were sufficient to justify a counterattacking volume, *The Critique of Humanism,* edited by C. Hartley Grattan and published in June, 1930.[1] Some of its contributors, like John Chamberlain, replied with an explicit defense of Brooks; others, like Edmund Wilson and Malcolm Cowley, did so implicitly by speaking the same arguments, even the same language Brooks had used in his earlier criticism of the humanists in *Letters and Leadership.*

Militant language, with a good deal of name calling on both sides, characterized the whole debate; an exchange of letters appearing in the *New Republic* (April 16, 1930) was appropriately captioned "At the Humanist Front." The controversy surged again with each new rebuttal. Norman Foerster returned to attack the Brooks-Bourne-Mumford leadership of the anti-humanists in his article for the *Bookman* (September, 1930), "The Literary Prophets." By the time it reappeared early the next year in Foerster's book, *Toward Standards,* however, the reiterated attacks on Brooks had worn thin; and Granville Hicks labeled Foerster's demonstration a "Swan Song." No one, after all, Hicks asserted with an air of finality, had set up "a more austere or more definite conception of artistic integrity than Brooks . . . ."[2]

Foerster, however, had made an important distinction which most writers overlooked in the heated defense of persons that occupied both sides. Brooks, Bourne, and Mencken were romanticists and therefore anti-humanists, said Foerster; but they were nevertheless in agreement with the humanists on the need for a creative use of the past. They disagreed chiefly over what past was to be used. The argument, in short, was over traditions. But the anti-humanists were so vocal in condemning the humanists for their reactionary preoccupation with the past and their evasion of present actuality that they slighted the appeal to tradition in Brooks's work. Only later, after Brooks's *Makers and Finders* volumes began to appear, did former anti-humanists and defenders of Brooks conclude that Brooks was also guilty of a refusal to heed the contemporary scene in favor of a more pleasant past. By then, some noted that even T. S. Eliot was not very far apart from Brooks.

For the moment, however, Eliot clearly appeared in the camp of the humanists. But his presence there posed something of a puzzle to some of the anti-humanists, especially among the more esthetic-minded writers who had taken their cues from the poetry and essays Eliot had written in the 1920's. To some of these *The Waste Land* was a masterpiece, but not even a humanist could call it a humanist masterpiece. Besides, Eliot's recent declaration that he was in politics a royalist, in religion an Anglican, and in literature a classicist—coupled with other recent pronouncements including his reservations about Irving Babbitt—suggested that he would go beyond Babbitt even. Eliot would call for a still higher check on man, that is, the authority of religion, of a church. To politically sensitive anti-humanists, Eliot was more to the "right" than Babbitt.

The line-up that ranged Brooks on the "left" as the real or original leader of the anti-humanists, and Eliot to the far "right," underwent an ironic reversal by the end of the decade when Brooks attacked Eliot.[3] Again, the reasons for this shift in literary leadership are complex but partly explained by the veering course that criticism in the 1930's followed in response to the ironies of history itself.

II   *The League and the Academy*

The controversy over humanism had already waned by the end of 1930 when Michael Gold, editor of the *New Masses* and one of the best spokesmen for the revolutionary left, turned the fracas into literary mayhem and shifted criticism in a new direction—away from the large abstract problems of morality, culture, and tradition posed by the humanists and toward concern for more immediate social and political issues. After the dust of the subsequent tumult had settled, the fundamental issue Gold had raised remained: *did* the American writer have "the artistic and moral right to turn his back on his times"?[4]

This question became a central one for writers during the rest of the decade. By and large American writers answered "No," but the nature of their answers ranged from those arguing the necessity of some detachment to those who made no distinction between artistic and moral responsibility and insisted on a total involvement of the writer in the revolutionary movement. *How* the writer acted on his responsibility made for endless debate and eventually endless cause for many a writer's going his own way. But for a while the economic and political crises of the early depression years, both at home and abroad, brought writers together who resolved in one way or another to exercise responsibility. The guild consciousness that came into being needed only the organizing energy of the Communist Party and willing fellow travelers to bring into actual existence, early in 1935, the League of American Writers.

Creature of the first American Writers Congress, held at the Mecca Temple in New York City on April 26, 27, and 28, 1935, the League was organized to enable writers to face two kinds of problems: those involved in devising effective political action to combat the twin dangers of war and Fascism, and those "peculiar to . . . writers, the problems of pursuing in their work the fresh understanding of the American scene"—that is, in a revolutionary context. The Congress elected Brooks's old friend Waldo Frank its first chairman, and among some thirty-nine other writers elected to its National Council was Van Wyck Brooks.[5]

Brooks's name was among those of twenty-two "well-known writers" who signed the call for the second National Congress that convened in New York City on June 4, 5, and 6, 1937. His name added some extra emphasis to the phrasing of the call: "Today in America there are signs of a literary revival that may resemble or surpass that of the period from 1912-1916—the period of the 'poetry renaissance' and the 'revolt against the genteel tradition.' Those of us who remember the hopeful activity of those years can also remember how it was cut short by the War. And we can see that the promise of the 1930's is threatened in a still more definite fashion."[6]

Reflecting some of the changes in Communist Party tactics since the inauguration in August, 1935, of the Popular Front, the Second Congress' declaration of the League's aims was couched in more general language, emphasizing culture over politics. The papers read at the Congress and printed in the published proceedings reflected the effort to enlist allies from those repulsed by the advances of Fascism in Germany, Italy, and Spain; and they showed also a conscientious attempt to place the contemporary revolutionary movement in an American tradition. In the course of the second effort, allusions to the earlier role of Van Wyck Brooks crept into several of the papers—in those by Joseph Freeman, Newton Arvin, Malcolm Cowley, and Granville Hicks. As the Congress closed, it elected Van Wyck Brooks to one of the seven vice-presidencies (to serve as chairman of the Connecticut writers) and announced the results of balloting among the League's members on the best books of the preceding year 1936, awarding *The Flowering of New England* the distinction for the best work of non-fiction.

The League provided several opportunities for writers to demonstrate at least an awareness of their involvement in the political actualities of the day. Conferences, organized regionally to meet in San Francisco, Chicago, New Haven, and elsewhere, gave many writers the chance to speak on public matters. From the conferences came resolutions, the formation of committees to investigate civil-rights cases involving writers, and fundraising campaigns to aid the Loyalists in Spain. Publicizing the solidarity of American writers in their opposition to Franco and Fascism, the League published its pamphlet, *Writers Take Sides: Letters About the War in Spain from 418 American Authors* (May, 1938). To Brooks's short statement that he was against Franco and Fascism and for the legal government and the people of Republican Spain, the editors appended a note about Brooks's contribution to the League's manuscript sale, organized for the benefit of the Medical Bureau to Aid Democracy (in Spain), which stated that the manuscript of *The Flowering of New England* had been auctioned for eight hundred dollars.[7]

The point of this recital of Brooks's associations with the League, the "official" body of writers on the left, is to illustrate one side of his public repute in the 1930's, a side that by and large was a projection into the revolutionary mixture of the younger literary radical of the 1910's and 1920's. The other aspect is seen in the increasing rise of his popular stature; for the approving reception by a larger "middlebrow" audience of *The Life of Emerson* and *The Flowering of New England*, his Pulitzer Prize, and his election to the American Academy of Arts and

Letters in November, 1937, marked his acceptance, finally, into the "official" world of literary respectability.

On the surface these two sides to the public image of Brooks seem contradictory. The Academy, for instance, was something of a traditional object of scorn by young writers, at least since the days of Mencken's assault on William Dean Howells, its first president; and it still bore the stigma of being a final resting place for the conservative mind of the country. The League perched defiantly at the opposite pole. Both groups, however, appealed to the nationalist sentiments of the 1930's. In its early days the League consciously sought to place the revolutionary movement in a national tradition. The Academy and the Pulitzer committees, while without political motivation in a narrow sense, were no less committed to enhancing the national cultural experience. In a few short years Brooks's associations with both groups would be scornfully recalled, but there were elements in his work which met with approval at both ends of the spectrum, and Van Wyck Brooks was important to the purposes of both.

When it later became evident that the Popular Front strategy of the Communist Party had exploited the "big names" for publicity purposes, Brooks and many others suffered disenchantment and then resigned. But initially, so long as the League emphasized its opposition to Fascism and its role in helping writers, it succeeded in attracting writers of every degree of reputation. For Brooks, participation in the League posed no dilemma at first. Like the Academy, it seemed to him primarily an instrument for creating a guild consciousness among writers. Though he was strongly anti-Fascist, he was opposed to the "mere political sitters-in," especially since the League would not condemn all dictators and dictatorships, Stalin as well as Hitler.

The contradictions in the League distressed Brooks, but he was patient. He could not altogether write off the "extraordinary unity of democratic feeling" and the sense the League gave to many writers that they were "members of a guild, a community, with vital ideas in common," the sense that had brought them together in the first place into organizations and leagues. It had been part of the "re-discovery of America by American writers" —to Brooks, the most inspiring fact of the 1930's. He would say so publicly, several times, even after he had become angered at the League's use of that sense of unity. But after the Nazi-Soviet pact and the League's coyness about taking a stand on the meaning of Soviet foreign policy, there could be little doubt about who ran the League. Brooks, along with many others, resigned —quietly, however, for he would not indulge in a public gesture that might encourage politicians, like those on the Dies Committee, to investigate the affairs of writers.[8]

III   *The Irresponsibles and Oliver Allston*

Brooks's old friends Lewis Mumford and Waldo Frank shared his qualities of mind and sentiment. Their angry-sad reflections on the failure of their generation to prepare the mind of America for the crisis posed by Fascism matched Brooks's growing sense of dismay and contributed to his response. Shortly after the Fascist armies marched, and after a period of searching reappraisal, Brooks put aside his labors on *Makers and Finders* to consider the American writer in the present in a mood reminiscent of the old days on the *Seven Arts*.

History—the rise of Hitler and Fascism, Stalin and Communism —made for an ironic difference, however. In 1917 Randolph Bourne had lashed out bitterly at intellectuals for supporting the "war-technique," for identifying themselves with the least democratic forces in American life, and for turning away from their espousal of neutrality. In 1940, Waldo Frank and Lewis Mumford, seconded soon by Archibald MacLeish and Van Wyck Brooks, accused intellectuals of failure in the opposite direction: they had rendered Americans apathetic before the threat of totalitarianism, they had contributed to the country's mood of isolationism, they had failed to make democratic ideals vividly real and worth fighting for. Bourne's words, as might be expected, were then ironically turned against his one-time associates for their own display of the new "trahison des clercs."

Archibald MacLeish brought the issue out of the political thicket and into a larger area for debate over literary and cultural issues and the relation of these to moral and political responsibilities. "The Irresponsibles," his label for the scholars and writers who had failed in their work to oppose the forces of oppression while they could, appeared in the *Nation* (May 18, 1940) within weeks after Hitler's invasion of the Low Countries. A second article, delivered first as a speech, "Post-War Writers and Pre-War Readers," appeared in the *New Republic* (June 10, 1940) as the German armies reached Paris and as Italy joined Hitler in the war. Against this demoralizing background of the collapse of the democracies before Fascism, MacLeish's soberly ironic accusations placed a special burden of guilt upon intellectuals.

Brooks responded in a manner characteristic of his younger days when he could cap his pessimistic judgment of the bleak state of affairs with a ringing note of affirmation that situations were about to improve. He found MacLeish's first article a moving statement that would "turn the tide in American literature" and "rouse our thinkers and set our intellectual world in action." That it did, and the first volley of replies from scholars and writers revealed widespread acknowledgment of the justice of MacLeish's charges and amounted to a kind of general confession of sin.[9] Opposition, indignant opposition, however, also soon appeared. Expectedly, while the Soviet-Nazi non-aggression agreement was still unviolated, the most angry replies came from the far left and in the *New Masses*.

During the Popular Front days MacLeish had been something of a "darling" to revolutionary writers. His popular successes with his radio dramas like *Panic,* and his official connections with the New Deal administration as Librarian of Congress had made him a valuable "well-known writer." But it had not always been so. In 1934 a *New Masses* writer had captioned a review of MacLeish's poems, "Der Schöne Archibald," and had flatly declared that "Archibald is a Nazi, at least a kind of ur-Nazi, whether he wants to be or not."[10] So it was not difficult for the *New Masses* to turn on MacLeish now, to call *him* "the Irresponsible," and to invoke the wrath of Randolph Bourne to castigate him as the real betrayer of the intellectuals. A series of *New Masses* articles in the fall and winter months of 1940 excoriated the "authors of surrender," "laureates of betrayal" and "the irrationals"—MacLeish foremost, but also Lewis Mumford for his "Mein Kampf," his "fascist-minded" *Faith for Living,* and Waldo Frank, Granville Hicks, Malcolm Cowley, Max Lerner.[11]

Although his friends Mumford and Frank received top billing along with MacLeish in the *New Masses'* counterassault, Brooks was not even mentioned. But on October 10, 1940, Brooks had delivered his address "On Literature Today" and had loudly seconded MacLeish's motion. MacLeish's first article, "The Irresponsibles," had been general in its indictment of scholars for their pretensions at scientific objectivity and consequent indifference to values—and of artists too for their seeing the world "as a god sees it—without morality, without care, without judgment." He mentioned not a single contemporary writer in this article, but in his second one he specifically named the writers of his own generation—not even sparing himself. Men like Dos Passos, Ernest Hemingway, Ford Madox Ford, Erich Maria Remarque, and Richard Aldington were singled out especially, for they had written books not only against the hatefulness of war, he said, but also with passionate contempt for belief in any ideals. When Brooks spoke, he cast an even wider net, snared more writers, and implied an even larger measure of responsibility for the "mood of desperate unhappiness" reigning in the world:

> The temperamental cards of our time are all stacked in favour of despair, and a somewhat sterile despair. One error that an optimist makes destroys his whole case, while a pessimist can get away with murder. It seems as if our writers passively wallowed in misery, calling it fate; as if the most powerful writers, from James Joyce to Hemingway, from Eliot of *The Waste Land* to Eugene O'Neill and Theodore Dreiser, were bent on proving that life is a dark little pocket. . . . You know the picture of life you find in the novels of William Faulkner, Dos Passos, James T. Farrell and so many others, who carry the day with their readers because they are writers of great power. They seem to delight in kicking their world to pieces, as if Civilization were all a pretence and everything noble a humbug.[12]

The following September, 1941, Brooks delivered another paper (at a Columbia University conference) that, having more sweeping and more biting judgments, made for wider repercussions. "Primary Literature and Coterie Literature," as he titled it, also extended his thesis on the literature of despair. He incorporated both papers in his *Opinions of Oliver Allston*, published in October, 1941; and the controversy over what was now called the "Brooks-MacLeish thesis" broke out with renewed intensity.

In *Opinions of Oliver Allston* Brooks was a revived "Henry Wickford," his alter-ego of the *Freeman* days. This mask and the book's strategy—purported excerpts from Allston's journal arranged topically, with comment on the journal entries and recalled "conversations" provided by a first-person narrator, Allston's "friend"—permitted Brooks to achieve a measure of objectivity in reviewing his own career and critical point of view. The book's objective, at the outset at least, was largely a personal, private motive. As his narrator says of Allston: "he might never have been driven to define himself if other critics had not attacked him." But what had commenced as an attempt to defend himself against the critics who had accused him of a "soft Emersonian idealism" or of retiring from the contemporary scene of letters to become a "scholarly story-teller" developed into a tirade, at times almost vindictive, against the main tendencies of contemporary letters.

There was much else in the book that was genial and urbane, and the portrait of Allston that emerges is one of a kind of eighteenth-century wit, capable of a good sense of humor about his own foibles. The self-portrait is amusing, showing a catholicity of tastes and preferences expressed in a wide range of quotations from the anthology of Western literature (though chiefly of the nineteenth century). There are candid notes about Allston's youthful ignorance of writers like Howells, whom he had attacked, and about his writing habits and "irritations." A wry comment about the characteristic "chip on the patriotic shoulder" of Allston is qualified by the assertion that he was nonetheless "culturally international—he loved a variegated world—the more it was diversified, the better." This much of the book had, in fact, already been released earlier in some nine installments in the *New Republic* from February 17 to August 11, 1941,[13] that had provoked no comment.

Except for frequent sniping asides at T. S. Eliot—in a book studded with references to literary figures, Eliot's name easily won the poll in the index—there was little hint of Allston's outburst to come. When it came, the speech on primary and coterie literature stole the show. It was reported in the press, and part of it published in the September *Yale Review*. When the book appeared, critical postures had already been taken on that part of the book, and the largely tolerant side of Allston went unremarked. In reviewing the rumpus over *Oliver Allston* it is difficult to avoid the conclusion that something like a guilty conscience, or anger stemming from blows delivered to sensitive areas of uncertainty, provoked the special acerbity of the replies. Although a genuine issue divided Brooks and his critics, a kind of willful perversity to distort Brooks's position set in and then grew into caricature.

No doubt the crisis-ridden background of events made acute the sensitivities of many intellectuals on guard against the siren appeals of anything smacking of chauvinism. The quarrel stretched out over the months just before and after the Japanese attack on Pearl Harbor, and this fact must partly account for the way many writers professed to see red, white, and blue at the mention of Brooks's name. But an equally strong tendency to make Brooks the archenemy of the creative process itself came from those with strong commitments to a view of literature as detached and above the movements of nations and the life that coursed beneath it.

Brooks's attack on "coterie literature" focused sharply on this view and the expression of it in the writing of the preceding years. The last half of the 1930's had witnessed a steady rise in the prestige of the "new criticism" even as the series of events which became a litany of disenchantment—the Moscow trials, the defeat of the Spanish Loyalists, Munich, the Nazi-Soviet pact, the fall of France—marked a decline in the dedication of writers to larger causes. Brooks called attention to a relationship between these upward and downward tendencies. Life and literature could not be considered separate and apart without each one suffering; to MacLeish's charge of moral irresponsibility, Brooks added that of artistic irresponsibility.

"Primary literature" and "coterie literature" proved to be inflammatory terms, igniting once again the central critical question which had crackled around Brooks's whole career: the nature of the artist's integrity and of the tradition from which it derived its strength. That strength came, Brooks affirmed, as could be seen in "primary literature"—the literature of greatness—from a fundamental faith in human progress that rested in turn upon faith in human nature and human goodness. Not "merely literary," it derived from "something quite beyond aesthetics," and from more than just the literature that had gone before. Writers drew strength from other writers but also from "a consciousness of human needs and longings; and their ultimate value was to be determined by the measure in which they responded to these longings and needs."

More importantly, literature grew out of and contributed to "the historic sense" as expressed, for example, in T. S. Eliot's statement about the writer's need for tradition—one which Brooks admired, he said, conceding his agreement in theory with Eliot on this matter. (Brooks relished turning his opponents' words against them to argue his own position, but it was a tactic others could use, and frequently did, against him.) Primary literature, in short, was positive, favoring the "life-drive" over the "death-wish"; the quality of the matter it informed was of first importance, its form only secondary; it grew out of the literature and life of one's own country, of Europe, of all mankind—in that order—composing a "simultaneous order" that made for tradition.

"Coterie literature" contrasted sharply with each of these criteria. Speaking the mood of the post-war years of the 1920's, such writing had reacted against the idea of human progress and had virtually denied it all together. It exalted form over matter. It appealed to tradition, but too often to a false tradition—one erected upon the personal impressions of the coterie leaders that succeeded only in destroying true tradition. So Allston returned to Eliot's definition, which, his "friend" said, Eliot had failed to sustain: ". . . the literature of his own country, the literature of Europe, the literature of all mankind, he said, composed for him a simultaneous order,—with the life of mankind, of Europe, of his country behind it. He began at home, with his own country, as the door through which to approach the classics, retaining the critical spirit, subjecting them to the proper tests, but accepting them, where one could, with one's whole heart."

The "coterie-writers," however, the "international mystagogues" —Pound, Proust, Paul Valéry, Gertrude Stein, along with Eliot and Joyce ("who had done more than Eliot to destroy tradition") —had, through the very "intensity" of their writing, dominated the literary scene for more than two decades. Their influence had affected "the whole of modern literature, led the dance in poetry, magnetized the novelists and overborne the world of criticism." The critics among them—they were rather "entomologists or geometricians" to Allston, with their "endless talk of technical matters" and their "famous symbolism"—possessed a special prestige. The "new criticism" had pre-empted the sphere of university critical study. Eliot was the new critics' "guardian angel," I. A. Richards their "John the Baptist." Contemplating the works of some of these critics—John Crowe Ransom, R. P. Blackmur, Cleanth Brooks, Yvor Winters—with their "Eliot clubs" in the universities, Allston confessed to a "blind rage":

> . . . if I resent these prestidigitators, it is largely on behalf of those who are younger than myself . . . younger sensitive minds who have had no other pabulum than these one-eyed writers, sickly adolescents, self-centred and neurotic, inexperienced per-

sons, divorced from the soil, divorced from their country, often, and from parenthood and love, ignorant of the general life, with no horizon beyond their noses or the spiritual slums in which they live. They are besotted egoists, one and all, stewing in their vanity, throwing dust in the eyes of their readers, mystagogues and swindlers. (248-49)

Clearly, here, at least, the scholarly gentleman had stepped aside for the angry moralist. "Kulturbolschewismus is here," announced Dwight Macdonald—in the non-Stalinist but still Marxist *Partisan Review*. A chain reaction followed. Brooks's speech at Columbia, Macdonald had written, was another sign of "the tendency to rally to the concepts of Hitler's (and Stalin's) 'new order.'" It was "a Dadaist gesture in reverse," employing the furious invectives of Dadaism but turned in defense of bourgeois-Philistine values. It was "the boldest statement to date of that cultural counter-revolution opened by Archibald MacLeish's attack on the 'irresponsibles.'" Brooks had become, "doubtless with the best intentions, our leading mouthpiece for totalitarian cultural values." In seeking, in effect, to purge writers like Eliot and Joyce, Brooks would kill a "living tradition" for the sake of "a sapless respectability."[14]

A typical *Partisan Review* symposium[15] followed in the next issue on the "Brooks-MacLeish Thesis." By this time, the United States was at war; and the editors, in disagreement still on the major political questions, announced that their main task would be to "preserve cultural values against all types of pressure and coercion." The "counterstatements"—from Allen Tate, William Carlos Williams, John Crowe Ransom, Henry Miller, Louise Bogan, James T. Farrell, Lionel Trilling, and, in a later issue still, T. S. Eliot—revealed general agreement with the editors that Brooks's attack had imperiled "cultural values." However, as might be expected of a group of individualists, each had his own particular grievance with Brooks.

The precise moment in history when Brooks made his attack on the dictatorial prestige of the "coterie-writers" made inevitable the countercharges, either directly or by implication, that Brooks had set off a Fascist-Stalinist purge of his own. Even T. S. Eliot's delicate reply professed to find in the social implications of Brooks's point of view a similarity to a reactionary position in England as expressed at the time in a London *Times* article, "The Eclipse of the Highbrow." Brooks's use of certain terms—

"the biological grain," "the life-drive," "race survival" (the last phrase, or variants of it, had been a talisman of Brooks's thought and style ever since his first critical book, which a younger Eliot had reviewed with favor)—seemed to Eliot "depressingly reminiscent of a certain political version of biology."[16]

Such political innuendoes soon became irrelevant, however, and in retrospect even absurd; a closer reading of Brooks's work would make equally absurd some of the sneers at his literary preferences. The real issue that divided Brooks from his critics remained. Of all the *Partisan Review* contributors, John Crowe Ransom came nearest putting his finger on it when he agreed with the substance of Brooks's generalizations but disagreed with Brooks's blaming the tendency of modern literature upon writers: "What Mr. Brooks should indict is not the writers, but the age which bore them."

The relationship of the writer to his times and the life around him was the issue. Those who assumed, like Brooks, a close intimacy between literature and life, and deduced therefrom the power of writers to give direction to life, to make civilization over as in a work of art, could expect no agreement from those who assumed otherwise. In Louise Bogan's words, "art, and its great power of enlightenment, truth-telling and release goes on . . . behind history's back."[17]

The controversy left its scars on Brooks's reputation and contributed in no small way to the half-hearted reception given to *Makers and Finders*. Few writers who contributed to the counterattack could avoid the temptation to rake over Brooks's whole critical achievement. The facile reiterations about his chauvinism, that he was "an official critic functioning in the behalf of an official literature," that he was at bottom a moralist and a Philistine without understanding of the esthetic emotion or the sense of tragedy, that he either lacked historical understanding or employed a false sense of the past that was ultimately "obscurantist and demagogic"—such assertions plagued him to the end of his career.[18] They bothered him enough to prompt him to reply, not directly, but in the pages of the last volume of his literary history. Read closely, the final chapters on "The Religion of Art" and "A Forward Glance" reveal answers to each of these charges; and he who recalls the turbulent years of the late 1930's and early 1940's may understand why Brooks still asserted the "liberal-democratic tradition" as the core of America's uniqueness.

CHAPTER 9

The Writer in America

BROOKS was sixty-five when he completed the last volume of *Makers and Finders*. For some twenty years he had followed a regular, rhythmical schedule of reading and writing, interrupted occasionally by journeys through the Middle West, to the Far West, and to the South in order to absorb more intimately the regions he was writing about. His work occupied him so completely that it might well have exhausted him. A different conception of the literary life might have brought him to a point of termination; had he not succeeded once before in facing up to and overcoming his personal malaise, he might have faltered again before other tragedies and disappointments. But it was almost literally true, as he told his friend Wheelock, that he could not breathe if he did not write.

He had engaged himself in the creation of a national memory. As the time scheme of *Makers and Finders* had moved toward the present, the lines of his personal memory were moving to meet it. Personal catastrophe like the loss of his wife, who died in August, 1946, sharpened by other personal losses about the same time in the deaths of close friends like Paul Rosenfeld, his associate from *Seven Arts* days, his Harvard classmate Edward Sheldon, and then Maxwell Perkins—all conspired to drive the present into the past even as he was bringing the past up to the present. The rest of his days were marked by a peculiar mingling of past and present, of meetings between the imaginative world of his makers and finders, and the real world—for Brooks also a world of writers and artists, of people connected in one way or another with "his" men and women.

After his wife's death, he moved to New York City. There, at Wheelock's apartment one day he met Gladys Rice and in June, 1947, they were married.[1] After a year or so of life in New York City, they sought the quiet of a country village and settled finally in 1949 in Bridgewater, Connecticut. The big white house they bought was on the village green and faced two churches and a small country store which was also the post office. A wide circular verandah swept around most of the house; and, with a large garden beyond, the whole setting suggested to Brooks a John Singer Sargent water color and the more confident times of fifty years before.

Outside, great beech trees spread protecting limbs over the house, and white birch, magnolias, and rhododendrons directed the line of sight from the verandah to the hills beyond. Inside, on the walls of the living room, a Yeats portrait of the young Brooks hung not far from Sargent's portrait of Gladys. In Brooks's study, across the wide hall from the living room, he lined the room to the ceiling with books—his own, many in translated editions from Italian to Korean and Japanese, as well as those of writers he could name as close friends. Soon the books accumulated in stacks on tables, on chairs, and on the floor, until the only safe place for the day's mail was a spot on the floor beside the chair of his writing desk. In these surroundings Brooks returned to the rhythm he had established for himself in previous years.

Bridgewater became at once home and a place to work. The tone of life there was mellow. Winters were sometimes spent in New York, once or twice in Cambridge. There were summer visits to Martha's Vineyard or Maine, or with the Wheelocks at East Hampton on Long Island. There were several trips to Europe: in the spring of 1951, a long visit to Ireland and England; in the spring of 1956, to Rome; and in 1959, to London and Edinburgh. Spring of 1955 found the Brookses in California; 1962, in Arizona. But the pace of life was leisurely. Wherever he went, work went with him. The tone of his writing increasingly matched the mellowness and leisure of his days.

At home, old friends among writers like Malcolm Cowley and Matthew Josephson lived nearby, as did Maxwell Geismar, Louis Untermeyer, Francis Hackett. Others were always dropping in. Away from home, there were writers too. In New York he saw something of Thornton Wilder, John Dos Passos, E. E. Cummings, and Stephen Vincent Benét; in California, Upton Sinclair, the Robinson Jeffers, Henry Miller, the Steinbecks. In Rome, it was 1956, Brooks could exclaim, "Half the young American writers are now turning up in Rome and we meet them all"— Theodore Roethke, Arthur Mizener, John Aldridge, and Ralph

Ellison among the Americans; Alberto Moravia, Ignazio Silone, Mario Praz among the other "multitudes of writers."[2] Whether at his writing desk, or in the garden, street, or drawing room, Brooks was constantly among writers. The writer in America was more than his subject; it was his way of living.

Two motives guided the work of his final years and gave a unity of purpose to what otherwise appears a miscellany of criticism, memoirs, biographical sketches, another long chapter in the history of American writers, and marginalia from his notebooks. Each miscellaneous bit, however, contributed another link among writers and threw out another line between past and present. Each grew naturally from the rich compost of his memory, now inextricably mixed with that of *Makers and Finders.* This motive he could not avoid. As he told Wheelock, "There always seems to be something to write about."

The other motive, just as necessary, accompanied the first: the need to justify the point of view which had dictated *Makers and Finders* in the first place. Although he was happy with his work, when it was going well, he was not content with the way it had been received. He was piqued and a little puzzled that the literary world of the 1950's still recalled and respected him chiefly for his role in the 1910's, while it neglected or minimized the chief effort of his later years. Despite the honors and awards given him, he did not miss, nor could he ignore, the tones of disparagement from other quarters that went with his being dismissed as a nostalgic storyteller or defender of mid-cult. Quite aside from the slight to him and what appeared sometimes a willful misunderstanding of what he had aimed at, he judged the neglect of his point of view as a symptom of the times that was understandable in its origins but, for Brooks, deplorable in its tendencies. Defending his own conception of the uniqueness of the American literary life, he wrote to check these tendencies.

I   A Final Defense

The momentum of the final chapters of *The Confident Years* carried Brooks into his next book, *The Writer in America* (1953). The trip to Ireland in the spring of 1951 had been intended, in part, to give him the ocean distance which would permit him to see America "from the outside again," somewhat as he had seen it when he wrote *The Wine of the Puritans* and *America's*

Coming-of-Age. The visit set off a whole chain of associations; and when he returned to Bridgewater that summer, he felt he had also returned to the mood and manner of those first books. "Makers and Finders," eventually the second chapter of *The Writer in America,* had been written first as an introduction to the five volumes of his history of the writer in America; but the effort became an apologia and then turned into an attack "on certain critics."

On the surface, the manner and mood and even the intent of *The Writer in America*—to arouse American writers to courage in the face of great odds, admittedly greater than those confronting them in the 1910's—were those of *America's Coming-of-Age.* Some of Brooks's targets were the same: professors and pedants, Puritans and esthetes (though the labels used for some of these had changed or had taken on slightly different overtones). He still pleaded the case of the amateur of letters, as against the professional, the too cerebral "scholar." An Emersonian point of view, essentially that of his earlier work, still informed nearly every page—an Emersonian insistence upon the priority of the individual will, a will that led from a basic faith in the forward movement of human progress.

Nonetheless, *The Writer in America* was a very different kind of milepost in American criticism from Brooks's earlier polemical essays. One difference was in tone and style—in the character and authority of the voice that spoke from its pages. Another resulted from the transformation that had occurred in the literary life in America between the 1910's and the 1950's.

The divided voice in *America's Coming-of-Age,* for example, one that spoke of Emerson as a personal possession forever, while another pugnaciously mocked Emersonianism in both the high and low reaches of America's mentality, was not the voice in *The Writer in America.* Here Brooks's voice was single, and his tone was quietly authoritative, not belligerently so. The rhetorical questions were those that allow room for qualified answers. A note of humility was frequent. Brooks posed a vigorous defense, but one markedly different from the offensive thrusts which had announced America's coming-of-age. Relying less, too, on his personal pronouncements, he revealed a consistent search for corroboration of his point of view from others; for he mustered an impressive array of quotations from other writers and critics—gleanings from his journals and notebooks like those he had published in *Opinions of Oliver Allston* and later in *A Writer's Notebook*. Some of the new notes came from the ranks of former opponents, like Paul Elmer More and Irving Babbitt; many came from contemporary and younger writers who might appear, at first thought, also among the ranks of the opposition, like *Partisan Review* critics Philip Rahv and William Phillips. Unlike *America's Coming-of-Age, The Writer in America* was not an American fable. Circumstances, as Brooks himself noted, often determine the forms that criticism assumes, and the changed circumstances in the American literary situation at mid-century had required new tactics.

Two circumstances primarily drew Brooks's fire: what he judged as the pernicious effect on writers of "a dominant critical 'pressure-group' with an almost despotic power," largely in academic circles; and the "unconscious" of the times which committed too many writers "to believe that man is the helpless victim of his own tendency to evil." Both these circumstances now seemed much more formidable than when he had first attacked estheticism and Puritanism. The "policy-makers" seemed everywhere entrenched in the universities, speaking the virtues of technique, craftsmanship and form. Literature had become highly specialized, and the gulf between highbrow and lowbrow in poetry and especially in criticism seemed even wider. The complacent optimism, Puritanism's twin in the 1910's, which had characterized the policy-makers of that bygone time, had been almost completely replaced in the highbrow circles of 1950 by its opposite, a complacency or resignation of despair, accompanied by a cynical negativism about the nation's culture where it was not altogether ignored. These were changes of degree rather than of kind, shifts of power in literary leadership. Assessing them, Brooks necessarily defended his own point of view which, if it encountered a different audience, now seemed more a consequence of these changed circumstances than of any change in himself.

The "despotic power" was, of course, that of the "new critics" whom he had lambasted in *Opinions of Oliver Allston*. He attacked them this time through a defense of his kind of literary history. Those who had rejected his *Makers and Finders* were the sort who insisted that a literary history must be a history of literary forms, a notion of literary history that underplayed the writer himself. Questions of literary form were vital, he said;

the new critics had added to criticism "a formidable dignity and weight" and had made it a power in the literary world "in which serious writers can all rejoice." But, had not this movement gone too far? Had it not, like the scholasticism of the Middle Ages, degenerated into "trivial displays of ingenuity" and lost its sense of "the content of thought" as it became more and more concerned with "the shells of form"? Above all, had not the new critics "ignored the larger bearings even of their own professions, for they seem never to have asked themselves how far their obsession with form is ultimately good for the writers who produced their texts."

For Brooks "the larger bearings" had always been those affecting the personality of the artist, and from first to last he had directed his energies to remove the obstructions impeding the artist's "natural growth." The new criticism, he felt, tossed up a number of obstructions. Its prepossession for technique obscured the truth that "form follows function." "Countless young writers," said Brooks, "think first of their form and . . . fit their material to a bed of Procrustes." Ignoring "their own temperaments and the visions of life that spring from these," they were "positively terrorized into writing as if metaphysics, and the forms of the metaphysical poets were native to them," or they followed the "preordained form of the fashionable master," Henry James, because James, "for obvious reasons, is a favourite of the critics." Under the sway of the new critics, writers too often pursued strange gods—masters of technique and craftsmen first; and masters of great subjects, the true criterion of great literature were second, if considered at all. Too often their gods were not "native" models but writers with whom they had nothing in common beyond form.

On this point Brooks returned to the defense of his purpose in *Makers and Finders* and resumed his feud with T. S. Eliot. As a favorite model of the new critics, Eliot offended Brooks on several counts: he was a formalist; he had worked "to restore the idea of tradition" but had "pointedly omitted from his conception of the wholeness of the past" nearly all of American literature, "the particular foreground of the past that was native to him"; and, finally, he had helped make fashionable again the idea of original sin. Brooks took issue, therefore, with each of Eliot's own avowals of himself as a classicist, a royalist, and an Anglican. Yet, long before Eliot had appeared to give forceful prestige to each of these positions, Brooks had quarreled with them. Except for a somewhat more reasonable tone, this view was not new in Brooks's work.

Similarly, the chapter "Beyond Adolescence" explored further the questions he had asked ever since *America's Coming-of-Age* regarding the complex fate of the American writer. Aborted talents were still too common, he said; but he was not willing now to assign writers' failings, as "when I wrote *The Ordeal of Mark Twain*," to external conditions—to their wives, friends, editors, publishers, or to the pressures of the world which may have destroyed them. Rather, "the talent is destroyed by writers themselves." Critics who refused to divert themselves from the question of "how to write well" to "how to live well to be a writer" only contributed to failures like those of Hemingway's writer-hero in "The Snows of Kilimanjaro." Writers needed to know "the art of literary living," and for this they needed to have models, "to have them on one's own terms, models, generally congruous with one's own conditions, who can illustrate the complex art of living as a writer and tell writers what they ought to know." This being so, American tradition was worth exploring "to find whatever models exist in the past"—not to shame the present with past examples, or to magnify the importance of writers like Hawthorne, Thoreau, or Emerson, or even to suggest that any one region, New England, for example, had a monopoly on good models, good caretakers of their talents, but more importantly so that American writers would "transcend the juvenile roles they so often perform." This concluding note matched the point Brooks had made in the concluding paragraph of *The Ordeal of Mark Twain*.

Placed alongside *The Wine of the Puritans* and *America's Coming-of-Age*, *The Writer in America* scarcely reveals a critic who had reversed or even modified his point of view in any important way. His experience with the critics of the past two decades, however, had taught him to buttress his expression of "faith in human goodness" with full confessions of his awareness of evil and tragedy in the world and of the justifiable reasons why men should falter. So a full chapter, "The Silent Generation," explored why so many contemporary writers shared "a renunciatory attitude" and "reasons . . . for the misery that weighs upon the modern mind." So too he revived the term and concept of "transnationalism" as first argued by his friend Randolph Bourne.

Brooks defined carefully his notion of "cultural nationalism" as having "little to do with politics or nothing whatever" and as implying no affirmation or defense of "the sadly different brazen world in which we spend most of our days." Mindful of his own earlier role in leading a rebellion against a brazen America, he defended "our drastic critical movement of thirty years ago" as both "warranted and salutary"; but he added that if it had had power to arouse so many writers it was because "so much warmth and faith lay, perhaps invisibly, behind it." His defense of nationalism turned out to be, he said, "In American terms, really a defence of Whitman's 'orbic' mind . . . ."

There were other increments, but no fundamental differences in his point of view of old. He had some new heroes, new "models" in his good friend Lewis Mumford, for one, to whom he devoted a full chapter as a "Prophet of Our Day," and in the art critic Bernard Berenson, with whom a mutual friendship developed as a result in part of this book. Albert Schweitzer was another, and even William Faulkner, "one of the paradoxes of our time" as Brooks called him, who "could write as he does of life and still defend so eloquently on a famous occasion not only the 'soul' of man but the 'duty' of the writer to lift men's hearts by reminding them of their courage, their honour, and their pride."

Nor was there any change or reversal in the final exhortatory words, a clear echo from *America's Coming-of-Age*, taking off in this instance from Faulkner's Stockholm speech: ". . . if writers could break the evil spell that weighs upon their minds they would write fully in that faith . . . for they would then be astride again of the instincts that are natural to them and that are paralyzed at present. It seems to me likely, in spite of appearances, that, in some future not too remote, we may look for some such transformation. For that way lies the line of human growth."

Although Brooks had tried to answer his critics of the previous two decades, he succeeded in tipping the balance hardly at all. Partly because *The Writer in America* did revive old issues, some readers greeted it with something like a yawn. The attack on the new criticism had about it an air of redundancy, and Brooks seemed to many to have overstated the extent of its power in academic circles, although this critical movement had effected a revolution in the teaching of literature. While the movement was, on the whole, a salutary one, it was not so pervasive or dominant as Brooks credited it to be. There were in fact, in the 1950's, signs of reaction in circles that had been influenced by it; moreover, some graduate schools of literature, for instance, seemed hardly touched by the new criticism and still emphasized a historical and philological approach to the study of literature.

Then too, despite Brooks's care to qualify and make considered reservations, his expression of faith in "goodness" to counter the prevailing pessimism and negativism of present-day writers caused others to wince. One reviewer wondered if the ghost of Irving Babbitt lurked behind Brooks's affirmation—a half-truth, surely; but even that half did injustice to both Brooks and Babbitt. The same reviewer confessed to "an uneasy" suspicion that "Mr. Brooks sometimes confuses virtues that make a good citizen or a good member of the state with those that make a fine writer."[3]

The pamphleteering tone of the book was partly responsible for this type of criticism. The tactics of the propagandist led often to overstatement; and outside the context of his many qualifying remarks and corroborating quotations, some of Brooks's statements seemed extreme. His defensive position could not hide the note of personal injury that lay behind much that he said. His references to Hemingway, F. Scott Fitzgerald (coming at a time when the revived interest in Fitzgerald was still soaring), to Faulkner, and to others could easily be read as injustices to each writer.

Yet, when all these factors have been considered, one concludes that the cool reception given Brooks may have been due in large part to the timing of his publication—a peculiar part of his fate since the late 1930's, but perhaps especially true of 1953. That year ushered in the comparatively complacent optimism of the "Eisenhower years" to the accompaniment of attacks on intellectuals and intellectualism, and it was also a time when nationalism took on an ugly aspect under the threatening cloak of McCarthyism. The anti-rationalism implicit in Brooks's romantic point of view and any defense of nationalism, even Brooks's careful delineation of his brand of transnationalism, might well have made for uneasiness. Moreover, the literary scene featured no contending critical camps and little of the sharp controversy over fundamental literary issues such as had marked the preceding decades. There were no rallying points either for opposition to or approval of Brooks's position. Finally, because it *was* Van Wyck Brooks, one of the older generation now and upon whom a stereotyped judgment had settled, he went largely unheeded.

All of this acknowledges some truth in Brooks's own contention that he wrote against the fashions of the moment, though they were more complex than he himself conceded. As the distance from that time lengthens and as historical perspectives on the American literary scene widen, it may even appear that *The Writer in America,* with the supporting weight of *Makers and Finders* behind it, marked the beginning of a change in the American literary climate—when what had reigned as "modernism," in criticism especially and in the poetry closely allied to it, often called "the Eliot tradition," was met, though not replaced by an equally vigorous movement advocating the "Whitman tradition."[4]

There would be fitting symmetry to Brooks's career if it should turn out that the critic who did much to rescue Whitman for the twentieth century at the outset of his career helped to do it again at the end of his career. It does not seem likely, however, for the new Whitmanians did not recognize an ally in Brooks. A time-gulf separated him from the newer generation; though they came together in a similar response to Whitman, the differences between them were almost those of the nineteenth as opposed to the twentieth century.

Brooks's closer affinity is still with Emerson, an Emerson who initially reacted spontaneously and warmly to Whitman, but did so with measured restraint thereafter. The new Whitmanians, concerned about asserting the equal vigor of the Whitman tradition in modern poetry alongside the more vocal domination of the Eliot tradition, have in turn their closer ties with the writers they advance—D. H. Lawrence, Hart Crane, William Carlos Williams, Henry Miller, and Dylan Thomas (though Brooks admired each of these writers too). These were writers who had found in Whitman a great release for their own talents and visions. Brooks responded to Whitman's worship of the soul; the new Whitmanians, to his worship of the body. Accepting Whitman at his word, both insisted on the identity of person and poem. But Brooks was interested ultimately in the personality, and he aimed at its evocation through the poem; the new spokesmen for Whitman, like Karl Shapiro and his colleagues, heirs of the Eliot tradition for all their attacks on it, are students of the Word and aim at the poem through the personality.

II *Final Connections and Confirmations*

The two motives—defense of his point of view, and the filling out of his world of makers and finders—continued to move Brooks's remaining work. The first motivation was less direct after *The Writer in America,* except for the memoirs and the published jottings from his notebooks (*From A Writer's Notebook,* 1958). He advanced his affirmations instead through his subjects, emblems often of the fulfilled personality who, like the blind Helen Keller, had triumphed over great obstacles through the sheer assertion of the will. *Helen Keller: Sketch for a Portrait* had been written at the request of Miss Polly Thompson, Helen Keller's companion, a request which stemmed in turn from the happy accident of Brooks's having been a Westport neighbor, one of Helen Keller's circle, along with his sculptor friend, Jo Davidson, who had first introduced Brooks to her. Yet her fame had already the proportions of a legend; and for Brooks, who had once pictured the American writer as a blind Samson shorn of his power, the tale of Helen Keller presented him with a ready-made, fabulous model of courage to set along-side that earlier image. As such he presented her; and since she had had numerous connections with writers and artists, she properly took her place among his other men and women.

Like so many of them, she was a model who corroborated Brooks's point of view, often even his own experience, as when Brooks observed that she might have said of herself that, "having learned the nature of evil, and admitted its power," she had turned "to the sun of goodness"; or that "she could not share [T. S.] Eliot's feeling that men were rotten, and her mind recoiled before the tomblike finality of *The Hollow Men,* although there was no denying the power of the poem"; or, finally, that Helen Keller, a modern saint, but not one of the fashionable saints of the day like "the cheerless creature in *The Cocktail Party,*" was a reply to "our fatalistic epoch" which, having "lost faith in the goodness of men, still recognizes the saints of the religion of art."

Similarly, *John Sloan: A Painter's Life,* while it stemmed directly from Brooks's personal connection with the artist, dating back to their days at Petitpas', and based in large part on Sloan's papers which Helen Sloan, his wife, had carefully assembled and turned over to Brooks, was also a corroborating portrait. The pattern of Sloan's intellectual life, as Brooks sketched it, resembled his own; and many of Sloan's attitudes and commitments —toward socialism, for example, or "art as a religion," artists as expatriates, and pride of country as a good influence on artists —were also Brooks's. Presenting the life of an American painter that was full of "human qualities," Brooks quietly advanced his own point of view.

The memoirs he had undertaken to write during these same years, partaking and sharing in the personal recollections involved in these books, advanced the same defense more overtly, but still quietly. The bemused, tolerant tone toward his adversaries and the image of his own earlier self suggest an old warrior who confidently expects vindication of the principal strategy behind his campaigns, even while confessing that occasionally (as in his opinion of Mark Twain, his thesis about Henry James, and his book on Emerson) he may not have been tactically sound in every respect. His own story was also emblematic: the story of a writer in America, in a world of writers and artists.

No less than in his *Makers and Finders*—to which the memoirs are an afterword and epilogue, overlapping and going beyond the years of the final volume—the emphasis was upon the many connections among writers moving in and out of Brooks's own life, all told with an air of wonderment that such fortune had been his, that others could possibly doubt the existence of an organic community of writers. There was much frankness about his early years, confessions of his ignorance and brashness, of his doubts and uncertainties, of his feelings that his work "had all gone wrong," about those years of nervous collapse when he was haunted in nightmares by the "great luminous menacing eyes" of Henry James. One wonders, in fact, what greater intimacies were expected by the reviewer who remarked that the memoirs were not "notably intimate."[5]

The intimate world of Van Wyck Brooks, the world he read about and wrote about, thought and talked about, was the world of the American writer, much like Brooks's imagined re-creation of the past; and the line between the actual world of his everyday life and the one he had lived in imaginatively was imperceptible. That line seemed non-existent to him. It does not seem likely that any deeper intimacies in his own life story will be uncovered that are any more notable than those he revealed, nor that they will alter this fundamental significance of Van Wyck Brooks the writer. The memoirs made abundantly clear how deeply he felt a personal involvement or connection with nearly every subject he wrote about. They were his intimacies.

III   *Arcadia and Howells*

Brooks measured out his life with printed pages of books. By the time he had completed his third volume of memoirs, taking his story down to his seventy-fifth year, he could include references to five books written since he had started his memoirs: the John Sloan and Helen Keller biographies, *From a Writer's Notebook*, and then, *The Dream of Arcadia*, his story of *American Writers and Artists in Italy, 1760-1915*, which is practically another volume in his *Makers and Finders*, and yet another biography, *Howells: His Life and World* (1959).

The dream of Europe, Italy in particular, as an Arcadia, had been Brooks's own as a young man. Frankly returning to "the feeling of enchantment" he had experienced in Italy as a boy, he wrote about Americans who had been driven by the same dream. Throughout his critical career, however, he had steeled himself against a superstitious evaluation of Europe and had warned others of its dangers. Now, confining his story to the years just before the exodus of writers and artists in the 1920's, he sought to recapture the enchantment in the experience of Americans before that period.

No charge of "rootlessness" entered these pages, and there was little hint of the consequences to artists who tore themselves from their native soil for too long.

In fact, he discovered evidence of a community of American writers and artists consisting chiefly of those who spoke their language—Byron and Landor, or Thackeray and Browning—or who had been driven from other countries by the same "time-spirit" to dwell for awhile in Italy. American writers, even when abroad, formed a distinct community. The final pages quickly spanned the twentieth-century years of expatriatism, the years when "the poetry of the Dream of Arcadia dwindled into prose"; but Brooks ended on his characteristic note of affirmation. A renewal was at hand: "How could there not be more travellers from a land where everything changed to the timeless world of the Pantheon. . . . In Rome, the Marble Faun still stood on the same spot in the same room where it had stood in the days of Hawthorne." Brooks was writing in Rome itself in 1956, and he spent his working days at the American Academy, living imaginatively with American writers of the past and encountering scores of American writers, members of the living community.

Howells: His Life and World grew as naturally from the last book and from Brooks's preoccupation with his own past as each of his previous books had led one to the other. Howells too had been a lover of Italy, and he had figured prominently in *The Dream of Arcadia*. In addition, Brooks had had a personal connection with him. Their lines had crossed as the one had embarked on his career while the other's slipped into decline. To some extent, Brooks had contributed to the neglect and then the contemptuous dismissal of Howells, his fate after 1920. Brooks had, since then, frequently confessed his earlier ignorance of Howells' work and had given Howells ample treatment, just and tempered, in both *New England: Indian Summer* and *The Confident Years*. The biography, however, amounted to payment in full.

Brooks attempted no definitive biography, but the completed work was the most rounded estimate of any one writer he had studied. It provided, in fact, a far better "synthesis" than did *The Life of Emerson* to the thesis and antithesis of Brooks's Twain and James studies. In presenting the story of a writer who had successfully maneuvered his art between the enchanting pull of Europe and the domineering energies of America, Brooks demonstrated that Howells had fallen prey to the extremes of neither. When Brooks went to some pains to redress old grievances once leveled against Howells, he found, for instance, that it would be "difficult to implicate Howells in what Santayana was to call the 'genteel tradition,'" for Howells had not been afraid to confront "the ugly realities, the surviving savageries, that the sunny hypocrisy of civilization denies." Brooks also quietly adjusted the scores he had once totaled up against Mark Twain and Henry James.

Brooks did not interrupt his narrative voice to point it out, but as he wrote of the older Howells, the personal lines of connection with Howells moved more and more between nearly parallel points. He must have enjoyed the irony, for instance, in discovering that Howells had been dismayed "that young people were taking up literature as a business"—about the same time that a younger Brooks had been appalled at the same tendency. Without enjoyment, but surely with some ironic thought of his own present position, he noted how Howells recalled the praise that had come his way when he was young, then the "scornings and buffetings from every side," and then, as Brooks put it, "with age came a relaxing, a withdrawal of this censure, a compassionate toleration followed, or the contempt of indifference; it no longer mattered to the world whether one worked well or ill, and then came the most perilous days of one's years. Then one felt tempted not so much to slight one's work as to spare one's nerves . . . to let a feeble performance blight the fame of more strenuous achievements in the past."

Brooks himself surrendered to no such temptations. Like Howells, he gave his hand over to the writing of prefaces, journeyman's work, but with no feeble performances among them, and he also joined in the paperback revolution that was helping to make American traditions available—part of his lifelong effort as a critic. Howells had been feted at his seventy-fifth birthday, and Brooks too enjoyed the homage of friends and contemporaries at a special dinner of the American Academy of Arts and Letters honoring his seventy-five years. Like Howells, he returned home to get back to work, not content to rest on the laurels tossed his way. He had time left for one more book.

Fenollosa and His Circle, With Other Essays in Biography was published in the summer of 1962. Each essay focused upon some figure he had touched on before who had moved through his *Makers and Finders.* These writers had intrigued him initially, and he had continued a search to find out more about them. He had uncovered some new materials about Ernest Fenollosa and, in one of those fortunate personal meetings that sometimes occur on shipboard, some unpublished and previously unknown correspondence of Fanny Wright's had been brought to his attention and subsequently made available to him. To these he added essays on other figures who in one way or another presented models of the planetary consciousness of the American writer.

Each essay appears unrelated, but each biography threw out another line of connection between America and other lands or other cultures: Fenollosa, with Edward S. Morse, Percival Lowell,

Henry Adams, John La Farge, and Lafcadio Hearn in Japan; the indefatigable traveller Fanny Wright and her dream of bringing the African Negro into a free relationship with the rest of the Western world; John Lloyd Stephens who pioneered in the archaeology of the Mayans, in Honduras and Yucatan; George Catlin, painter and student of the American Indians; Charles Wilkes, naturalist, explorer, and discoverer of the Antarctic regions and Pacific islands; Charles Godfrey Leland, who studied and wrote about the folklore of American Indians, of gypsies the world over, of the Italian witches of Tuscany; and finally, fittingly rounding out this collection, a new essay based on new materials besides his personal recollections, about his old friend Randolph Bourne who had struck out against America's "cultural humility" in the face of other civilizations and had proposed a new American nationalism. All of these, even the slight "Anecdotes of Maurice Prendergast," a republication from an earlier time, were essays in the transnationalism of American culture.

Brooks had one last opportunity to comment upon the writers of his own time in a preface to the second series of *The Paris Review* interviews, *Writers at Work* (1963). It was brief. The writers—Robert Frost, Pound, Marianne Moore, T. S. Eliot, Hemingway, Henry Miller, and others—spoke for themselves. Brooks merely noted some generalizations, but anyone familiar with his point of view could detect some of the tones of a vindicated critic.

"They are individualists," he said of these writers, "but one generalization seems quite clear, that there is little difference any longer between the American mind and the European." These writers seemed, he said, "to represent the one world toward which the modern mind is aiming." Most of them had wished to be writers from the first, but "they usually seem glad to talk of anything but the business of writing." Ezra Pound, he noted, "has replaced his interest in form with an interest in content," and the others too preferred "to discuss their subjects rather than their form." Of T. S. Eliot, his old *bête noire*, he had only a laconic comment to make: Eliot believed he might have been handicapped as a writer had he not had to bother about earning a living—he had had to contend with the art of literary living. Finally, still interested in connections, Brooks observed how "odds and ends of autobiography" in the interviews "now and then bring these writers together." Though individualists, they formed a community of writers.

After *Fenollosa*, he had planned at least two longer studies of contemporary writers, younger contemporaries of his: one, of his friend Lewis Mumford, about whom he actually completed drafts for two chapters; another of his fellow critic, Edmund Wilson. But time had run out. In the late summer of 1962 he suffered a stroke and underwent surgery. Recovery was slow. A second sojourn in a hospital uncovered an old ailment and necessitated surgery again. He lingered on, increasingly enfeebled in body but strong in will and insisting on a daily visit to his working study, until on May 2, 1963, he died.

IV *Conclusion*

Van Wyck Brooks's contribution to American literature was twofold. Both contributions were idealistic, both were "prophecies of possibilities."[6] One was his vision of artistic integrity, of the importance of the writer's being true to his own inner genius; the other was his vision of an ideal community of writers and artists, of an American tradition which provided a kind of spiritual resource for individual American artists. He made both contributions in the course of a long career dedicated to puzzling over what it meant to be an American artist.

His historic role as a "literary radical" is of first importance. Few have questioned the priority of his critical leadership in helping to launch "modernism" in American literature. Irving Howe, who expressed little sympathy for Brooks's social approach to literature, and none at all for Brooks's later work, nevertheless felt that the beginnings of a distinctly "modern" criticism in America could be dated precisely: 1915, the year Brooks published *America's Coming-of-Age*.[7] On this role, there is wide agreement.

How Brooks asserted his leadership is not so clear, and less certainty prevails in assessing the nature of his leadership. He provided American critics with no coherent set of ideas about literature; no distinct techniques for the analysis and judgment of a poem or a novel; no clear criteria, even, on how to judge an artist's success or failure. His identification of personality with form was, perhaps, a pace-setting idea for much subsequent biographical criticism. In handling the theme of the alienated artist he brought into the literary scene of the 1910's and 1920's a heightened awareness of the pressures imposed on art by an industrial, commercial, mass society, and he provoked others into examining the effects of these pressures on art and the artist.

However, it was not his ideas, which were few and broad, so much as a tone and a style, and an ability to invoke usable images and myths—his establishment, in short, of a distinct attitude toward literature as a guiding force in civilization—which he contributed toward the making of modern American literature. It was the quality of his critical voice, raised at the right historical moment and insisting that "artist" and "American" need not be contradictory terms that persuaded Brooks's early audience to believe in a higher organized life of art for America. He pointed to a possibility, and gave courage to other American writers.

On the value of his second major contribution there is considerably less agreement, even widespread uneasiness that his idealization of the American literary past is dangerous, an invitation to misplaced pride and complacency. A prophecy of what might be is one thing; a prophecy of what has been is a paradox. Yet Brooks's ideal community of writers and artists, abstracted from the record of the American literary imagination, was intended by him as a model—an example of the possible—and must, therefore, be taken as a species of prophecy. Approached as such, his ideal community has the same power to goad the imagination as did his earlier criticism. There are dangers in prophecy, no doubt, but to take an Emerson too literally, after all, has always been risky.

Brooks's later work either inspired or irritated his readers, and both reactions can have valuable consequences. In either event, the debt to Brooks's historical imagination remains a large one. As Edmund Wilson has pointed out,[8] Brooks was the first modern literary historian to go over the whole ground of American literature from its national beginnings. He succeeded, moreover, in modifying the order of monuments in the American past, and he brought new light onto half-buried resources. In a rare combination of the literary prophet with the literary scholar, and in the tradition of European literary historians like Taine and de Sanctis, he wrote literary history as an art form itself. With a distinctly Emersonian grasp of the artist as a whole person, Van Wyck Brooks was a maker and finder himself, a part of the community he imagined was possible.

Notes and References

Chapter One

1. Brooks's memoirs appeared originally in three volumes: *Scenes and Portraits: Memories of Childhood and Youth* (New York, 1954); *Days of the Phoenix: The Nineteen-Twenties I Remember* (New York, 1957); *From the Shadow of the Mountain: My Post-Meridian Years* (New York, 1961). I have drawn from the first of these for my account of his early years; unless otherwise noted, quoted phrases and references to Brooks's recollections are from *Scenes and Portraits*. The three volumes were republished as one, called *An Autobiography* (New York, 1965).

2. Many years later, when a Mr. Delafield, an enterprising bibliographer of the poet Wheelock, persuaded Brooks to dig out a copy of *Verses* from his attic, Brooks did so with his customary generosity, but with mixed pleasure and pain. Wheelock was the poet, he said, and he was pleased that his friend was getting the recognition he deserved, but the "relics" from his own past did not make him particularly happy. Letter, Brooks to Wheelock, n.d. (probably June, 1952). This and other letters to and from Brooks in the Brooks Collection at the Library of the University of Pennsylvania, quoted with permission of Gladys Brooks and the Library of the University of Pennsylvania.

3. Letter dated December 26, 1906, under the letterhead of the New York *Evening Post*, addressed to Mr. [Frank Moore] Colby. Quoted with permission.

4. Brooks's interview, "Mr. Howells at Work at Seventy-Two," *World's Work*, XVIII (May, 1909), 11546-49. The letter, Howells to Brooks, May 7, 1909, is quoted with permission. See also *Opinions of Oliver Allston* (New York, 1941), p. 22.

5. See "John Butler Yeats," in *Emerson and Others* (New York, 1927), and in *Sketches in Criticism* (New York, 1932). Also in Brooks's biography, *John Sloan: A Painter's Life* (New York, 1955), and in *Scenes and Portraits*.

6. Brooks attributed this to Sainte-Beuve's influence—"even perhaps his weakness in making all his characters 'six feet tall' "—and acknowledged indebtedness to Irving Babbitt. *Scenes and Portraits*, p. 122. Of Sainte-Beuve Babbitt wrote that he "exercises his incomparable gift for psychological biography with at least as much complacency on second-rate as on first-rate writers." *Masters of Modern French Criticism* (Boston and New York, 1912), p. 165. See Edmund Wilson's similar complaint about Brooks's *The Flowering of New England* in Wilson's *Classics and Commercials* (London, 1951), p. 12 and p. 230.

7. Stanley Edgar Hyman, *The Armed Vision* (New York, 1948), p. 122. Cowley's comparison is in his essay, "Van Wyck Brooks at

75," *Saturday Review*, XLIV (February 18, 1961), 15. Earlier, Cowley had said the same thing of *The Ordeal of Mark Twain* in "Brooks's Mark Twain: Thirty-Five Years After," *New Republic*, CXXXII (June 20, 1955), 17-18, reprinted as the introduction to the Meridian Paperback edition of *The Ordeal of Mark Twain* (New York, 1955). Robert E. Spiller has made the same comparison in his essay, "Literature and the Critics," *American Perspectives: The National Self-Image in the Twentieth Century*, ed. Spiller and Eric Larrabee (Cambridge, 1961), p. 37.

8. Brooks's "Introduction" to Bourne's *The History of a Literary Radical* (New York, 1920), a posthumous publication of essays.

Chapter Two

1. Two manuscripts, never published, preceded and then went into the final book. The first, "Imaginary Letters," Brooks had completed at Harvard in June, 1906, and consisted, as its title suggests, of a series of "Letters"—"From a critic to a poet," "From a victim of the Literary Temperament to an artist," "From an artist in Italy to a Philosopher," and so on. The second, written in England, was a first-person account covering the same themes, and entitled "What is America?" *The Wine of the Puritans* was a merger of these two earlier attempts.

2. Frederick W. Dupee, "The Americanism of Van Wyck Brooks," *Partisan Review*, VI (Summer, 1939), 69-85. Reprinted in volume II, *Literary Opinion in America*, ed. Morton Dauwen Zabel (Harper Torchbooks, 1962).

3. Paul Rosenfeld, *Port of New York: Essays on Fourteen American Moderns* (New York, 1924), p. 21.

4. There is, of course, a significant difference in these two positions which accounts even more for the subsequent divergence of the two men. Despite his use of the phrase "ideal order," Eliot is more the relativist here than is Brooks, suggesting that it is the contemporary work which changes our judgment of the past, making a John Donne, for instance, more important for a while, than a John Milton. Brooks looks in the other direction, from past to present, giving more absolute authority to the past and its power to modify the contemporary work.

5. *The Soul: An Essay Towards A Point of View* (San Francisco, 1910). The longer passage, p. 10.

6. Earl H. Rovit, "American Literature and 'The American Experience,'" *American Quarterly*, XIII (Summer, 1961), 115-25.

Chapter Three

1. Brief portions of *The Malady of the Ideal* had, however, appeared in the *Forum* prior to book publication: "Maurice de Guerin," *Forum*, XLVII (May, 1912), 621-28; "Amiel," *Forum*, XLVIII (July,

1912), 120-28. Similarly, preceding book publication was the short essay "John Addington Symonds," *Forum*, XLIX (April, 1913), 489-500. Brooks published at least two other essays in the *Forum:* "Notes on Vernon Lee," XLV (April, 1911), 447-56; "Platitude," XLVIII (November, 1912), 608-11.

2. *The Malady of the Ideal* (Philadelphia, 1947), p. 86.

3. See Louis Fraiberg, "Van Wyck Brooks versus Mark Twain versus Samuel Clemens," *Psychoanalysis and American Literary Criticism* (Detroit, 1960). The first English translation of Freud appeared in 1913, the same year as *The Malady of the Ideal,* but too late for Brooks to have used it. In 1918 he discovered Bernard Hart's *The Psychology of Insanity* (1912), a more immediate source than Freud for his studies of Twain and James.

4. *John Addington Symonds: A Biographical Study* (New York, 1914), pp. 28-31.

5. *The World of H. G. Wells* (New York, 1915), pp. 181-83.

6. *America's Coming-of-Age* (New York, 1958), p. 4. Page references hereafter given in text, all to this Doubleday Anchor edition.

7. William Graham Sumner, "Politics in America, 1776-1876," *North American Review*, CCL (January, 1876), 54-55.

8. To cite only a few: Vernon Louis Parrington's *Main Currents in American Thought* (New York, 1927), whose title may have derived from the paragraph quoted (Brooks was the reader for Harcourt, Brace & Company, and urged publication of Parrington's work), is one detailed examination of Brooks's outline. More recently, R. W. B. Lewis' *The American Adam* (Chicago, 1955) in its account of nineteenth-century American literature resulting from a dialogue between the Voice of the Past and the Voice of the Future seems to me a sophisticated extension of Brooks's thesis. Richard Chase, in *A Democratic Vista* (New York, 1958), revived Brooks's terms to explore the way the tensions between Brooks's two extremes accounted for the unique features of American literature. Randall Stewart, in *American Literature and Christian Doctrine* (Baton Rouge, 1958), even writes of Franklin and Edwards: ". . . these two giants divided between them the American eighteenth century, and they have divided America and the American mind between them ever since." I find the linked phrases of "high ideals" and "catchpenny realities" constantly recurring in contemporary scholarship, sometimes to point out an earlier "germ" of Brooks's insight (Alan Trachtenberg, "The Rainbow and the Grid," *American Quarterly*, XVI, Spring, 1964) or to argue the need still to "unify our individual and social universe" (Max Lerner, "Notes on Literature and American Civilization," *American Quarterly*, XI, Summer 1959, Part 2).

Chapter Four

1. Stuart P. Sherman, "The Battle of the Brows," *Nation*, CII (February 17, 1916), 196-97. Sherman's review of Brooks's study of Wells

first appeared in the *Nation*, C (May 20, 1915), 558-61, and was included along with Sherman's review of Wells's *Mr. Britling Sees It Through* under the title, "The Utopian Naturalism of H. G. Wells," in Sherman's *On Contemporary Literature* (New York, 1917).

2. *Dial*, L (April 1, 1911), 251.

3. See James Oppenheim, "The Story of the Seven Arts," *American Mercury*, XX (June, 1930), 156; Paul Rosenfeld, *Port of New York* (New York, 1924), p. 48. Frank's letter to Brooks, undated, quoted with permission.

4. "The Critics and Young America," in *Criticism in America: Its Function and Status*, ed. J. E. Spingarn (New York, 1924). Except in the instance of this revision and where noted elsewhere, I have quoted from *Letters and Leadership* as it appears in the Doubleday Anchor edition of *America's Coming-of-Age* (New York, 1958), a reprint of *Three Essays on America* (New York, 1934) published by E. P. Dutton & Co., Inc., to whom I acknowledge thanks for permission to quote. Page references in parentheses after long passages are to the Anchor edition.

5. Brooks deleted in revision the phrase "incredulous pedagogues" and the sentence calling his remark "a merciful epitaph." They will be found in the 1918 *Letters and Leadership*, pp. 91-92.

6. Foerster's letter to Brooks, April 5, 1919, quoted with permission.

7. Bourne's letter to Brooks, March 27, 1918, printed in full in *The World of Randolph Bourne*, an anthology edited and with an introduction by Lillian Schlissel (New York, 1965), pp. 316-21.

Chapter Five

1. Letter, Frank to Brooks, November 27 (1918), quoted with permission. Bourne's phrase is from his letter to Brooks, March, 1918, printed in large part in Louis Filler, *Randolph Bourne* (Washington, D.C., 1943), pp. 121-22, and more recently in full in Lillian Schlissel (ed.), *The World of Randolph Bourne* (New York, 1965), pp. 315-16. In this same letter Bourne wonders if Brooks will not revise his judgment on Twain, and he confesses to feeling "a holy mission" to convert Brooks to *The Mysterious Stranger* in which Bourne saw "as blinding satire on the human comedy as anything Swift ever wrote." Page references to *The Ordeal of Mark Twain* are from the Meridian Books edition, reprinted by arrangement with E. P. Dutton & Co., New York, 1955.

2. Randolph Bourne, "Traps for the Unwary," *Dial*, LXIV (March 28, 1918), 277.

3. Frederick J. Hoffman, *Freudianism and the Literary Mind* (New York, 1949), p. 52.

4. *Freeman*, II (December 15, 1920), 335.

5. Malcolm Cowley, "Brooks's Mark Twain: Thirty-Five Years

After," *New Republic,* CXXXII (June 20, 1955), 18. Robert Morss Lovett, "An American Morality," *Dial,* LXIX (September, 1920), 299. For evidence of how at least one writer gained some courage from *The Ordeal of Mark Twain* see F. Scott Fitzgerald's letter to Maxwell Perkins, n.d. [before December 12, 1921] in *The Letters of F. Scott Fitzgerald,* ed. Andrew Turnbull (New York, 1963), p. 150.

6. For an excellent summary of the controversy see Lewis Leary's essay, "Standing with Reluctant Feet," in *A Casebook on Mark Twain's Wound,* ed. Leary (New York, 1962), pp. 3-32. The *Casebook* reprints long excerpts from the original 1920 edition of *The Ordeal of Mark Twain* and a number of the early reactions to it.

7. "Introductory Note" to Sherwood Anderson's "Letters to Van Wyck Brooks," in *The Shock of Recognition,* ed. Edmund Wilson (New York, 1955), p. 1257.

8. *Days of the Phoenix* (New York, 1957), p. 174.

9. As reprinted in *Three Essays on America* (New York, 1934), reissued as a Doubleday Anchor paperback entitled *America's Coming-of-Age* (New York, 1958), pp. 166-67.

10. *Dial,* LXIV (April 11, 1918), 337-41.

11. Letter, Spingarn to Brooks, December 23, 1921, quoted with permission.

12. *Freeman,* II (November 24, 1920), 262.

13. *Bookman,* LXII (October, 1925), 156.

Chapter Six

1. Letter, Cowley to Brooks, December 18, 1923, quoted with permission.

2. For the *Dial* offer to Brooks, and a discussion of Brooks's influence on the *Dial,* see William Wasserstrom, *The Time of the Dial* (Syracuse, 1963), p. 110. Brooks himself told me of the other offers made to him. The Sherman reference is from Sherman's letter to Brooks, April 18, 1926, quoted with permission.

3. The quoted phrases are from the final chapter, "A Season in Hell," in Brooks's *Days of the Phoenix: The Nineteen Twenties I Remember* (New York, 1957).

4. Edmund Wilson, "Van Wyck Brooks's Second Phase," *New Republic,* CIII (September 30, 1940), 452-54, reprinted in Wilson's *Classics and Commercials* (London, 1951). Bernard De Voto, *The Literary Fallacy* (Boston, 1944), p. 62.

5. See Anderson's letters to Van Wyck Brooks in Edmund Wilson's *The Shock of Recognition* (New York, 1955), especially p. 1261. Bernard Smith, "Van Wyck Brooks," *New Republic,* LXXXVIII (August 26, 1936), 69-72. Robert E. Spiller, "The Battle of the Books," *Literary History of the United States,* ed. Spiller *et al.* (New York, 1948), II, 1140.

6. The "Others," filling out half the book, consisted of essays that had been published elsewhere: "The Literary Life in America" and "Randolph Bourne," and from the *Freeman* the essays on "John Butler Yeats," "The Letters of Ambrose Bierce," "Amor Fati" (on writers developing a "craft sense"), "Notes on Herman Melville," and "The Novels of Upton Sinclair." Of these last essays, the most noteworthy is the "Notes on Herman Melville," wherein Brooks, in a pioneering essay in the Melville revival, judged Melville a truly great writer, a natural artist, who had fashioned *Moby Dick* with a careful, deliberate art.

7. Review by Morris U. Schappes in *The Symposium*, October, 1932, pp. 540-47. Among those calling it "a poem" were Howard Mumford Jones, in the *Virginia Quarterly Review*, VIII (July, 1932), 439-42; Ralph L. Rusk, in *American Literature*, V (March, 1933), 70-72; and James Grey, *St. Louis Dispatch*, April 6, 1932.

8. See p. 80, the original 1915 edition. As noted in Chapter III, Brooks deleted this phrase in revision in order to lessen the apparent contradiction in his giving the same primary role to Whitman. The contradiction remains implicit in revision, however. Compare p. 43 and p. 59, the Doubleday Anchor edition.

Chapter Seven

1. Dwight Macdonald, one of the first to so charge Brooks—see Chapter VIII—reiterates it still. See his essay, "By Cozzens Possessed," reprinted in Macdonald's *Against the American Grain* (New York, 1962), p. 208.

2. But, Brooks added, anticipating the rediscovery of his own generation: "Emerson's words were written on the walls of the nation," and if they became overlaid, "as the walls of a house are overlaid with fresh layers of paper," in decades to come whenever "the house was renovated and the old layers of paper were stripped away, those words came to light again; and America once more saw the star of promise first seen in its early morning." *New England: Indian Summer* (New York, 1940), pp. 59-60.

3. Edmund Wilson, "Van Wyck Brooks on the Civil War Period," *New Yorker*, XXIII (November 29, 1947), 130-38, reprinted in Wilson's *Classics and Commercials* (London, 1951).

4. Bernard De Voto, *The Literary Fallacy* (Boston, 1944), pp. 74-84. I have paraphrased what De Voto said of Brooks's treatment of Longfellow when De Voto asked: "Did he not feel, hope, suffer, and despair much more intensely than he is permitted to in the exquisite colors of Mr. Brooks's prose?" (p. 78).

5. Edmund Wilson, "Van Wyck Brooks's Second Phase," in *Classics and Commercials*, p. 12.

6. Lionel Trilling, "A Young Critic in a Younger America," review

of Brooks's *Scenes and Portraits* in the New York *Times Book Review,*
March 7, 1954, p. 28.

7. Lewis Mumford, "Our Rich Vein of Literary Ore," review of
The Times of Melville and Whitman in *Saturday Review of Literature,*
XXX (November 8, 1947), 13.

8. F. O. Matthiessen, "Pilgrimage to the Distant Past," New York
Times Book Review, October 1, 1944.

9. See Trilling's essay, "Reality in America," in *The Liberal Imagination* (New York, 1953), p. 20. The later quotation is from Trilling's
review of *Scenes and Portraits,* cited above.

Chapter Eight

1. A third "symposium," not usually counted as part of the humanist controversy, should nevertheless be considered: *I'll Take My
Stand: The South and the Agrarian Tradition,* by "Twelve Southerners"
(New York, 1930). Allen Tate, for one, appeared as a contributor
in it and in *The Critique of Humanism,* but there are other points of
connection.

2. Malcolm Cowley and Edmund Wilson, then both editors of
the *New Republic,* had in earlier issues contributed lengthy essays
attacking the humanists. See Wilson's "Notes on Babbitt and More,"
New Republic, LXII (April 9, 1930), 207-11. In the issue of March
26, 1930, the Correspondence column (p. 153) included a brief ironic
request: "Wanted: A Humanist Masterpiece," signed by thirty-three
writers. The Correspondence entitled "At the Humanist Front" was
largely in reply to these earlier pieces, with Frank Jewett Mather, a
contributor to *Humanism and America,* proposing Paul Elmer More's
Shelburne Essays as a "Humanist masterpiece," and Seward Collins,
editor of the *Bookman,* a humanist journal, taking bitter issue with
Cowley for what he had taken to be Cowley's charge of anti-Semitism.
Cowley and Wilson each added rebuttals to these letters, neither
yielding an inch. Granville Hicks, "Swan Song," *The New Freeman,*
II (February 4, 1931), 499.

3. Brooks, in effect, accused Eliot of being a "literary dictator."
The implications of such a role were explored by Delmore Schwartz
much later in "The Literary Dictatorship of T. S. Eliot," *Partisan
Review,* XVI (February, 1949), 119-37. But as far back as 1924,
Mary M. Colum had said that Eliot's view of the function of the critic
was a plea "for . . . literary dictatorship." She added that it was
"the business of criticism to abolish literary dictators." Brooks, she
said, was "in no sense a dictator . . . but a pathfinder, a contributor
of transforming ideas." See "An American Critic: Van Wyck Brooks,"
Dial, LXXVI (January, 1924), 33-41.

4. See Gold's editorial in the *New Masses,* V (April, 1930), 4, and
his essay, "Wilder: Prophet of the Genteel Christ," *New Republic,*

LXIV (October 22, 1930), 267. See also Daniel Aaron's admirable recounting of "the Communist offensive against Humanism" in his *Writers on the Left: Episodes in American Literary Communism* (New York, 1961), pp. 237-43. The phrasing of the issue, quoted at the end of the paragraph is Aaron's, pp. 242-43.

5. See *American Writers' Congress,* ed. Henry Hart (New York, 1935). The Introduction, by Hart, gives in full the statement of "the call" issued to writers, and the names of the signers (10-12). Brooks's name is not among these. Page 188 lists the names of persons elected to various offices and committees.

6. The proceedings of the second Congress were published in *The Writer in a Changing World,* ed. Henry Hart (New York, 1937). The phrase "well-known writers" is used on p. 195 in listing the signers. The "call" itself follows on pp. 196-99. The references to Brooks occur on p. 18 (Freeman), p. 43 (Arvin), p. 46 (Cowley) and p. 180 (Hicks). The summary of the elections appears on pp. 254-56.

7. *Writers Take Sides* (New York, 1938), p. 9.

8. See *Opinions of Oliver Allston* (New York, 1941), pp. 128-31, where Brooks reproduced parts of the actual letter he wrote to Malcolm Cowley announcing his resignation and the reasons for his rejection of the League. See also *From the Shadow of the Mountain* (New York, 1961), p. 85, for further recollections by Brooks on his frustrating relations with the League.

9. Brooks's reaction was expressed in a letter to the editors, *Nation,* CL (June 8, 1940), 718. See the letters in the *Nation,* CL (June 1, 1940), from Max Lerner, Kenneth Murdock, Waldo Frank, Hans Kohn, Waldo Leland, Perry Miller, Joseph Freeman, Willard Thorp. All but Freeman expressed agreement with MacLeish, Waldo Frank strongly so. Freeman declared that it was an "illusion" of writers that their words had power.

10. Margaret Wright Mather, "Der Schöne Archibald," *New Masses,* January 16, 1934, p. 26.

11. Samuel Seldon, "Archibald MacLeish, the Irresponsible," *New Masses,* June 11, 1940, pp. 24-26; "Authors of Surrender," *New Masses,* October 8, 1940, pp. 4-7; "Lewis Mumford's 'Mein Kampf,'" *New Masses,* October 15, 1940, pp. 8-10; "The Irrationals," *New Masses,* October 29, 1940, pp. 20-22; "The Choice Before Us," *New Masses,* December 3, 1940, pp. 17-18.

12. The passage quoted is from *On Literature Today* (New York, 1941), pp. 14-15. It was delivered first as a speech at the inauguration of Dr. George N. Shuster as president of Hunter College. "Primary Literature and Coterie Literature" was first delivered as a paper at the Second Annual Conference on Science, Philosophy and Religion held at Columbia University, New York City, September 10, 1941.

13. Brooks's name had been listed as a "contributing editor" for

the *New Republic* in the issue of February 3, 1941. His name continued to be so listed until January 8, 1945. The nine installments of *Allston* were the first nine chapters. "What is Primary Literature?" first appeared in the *Yale Review*, XXXI (September, 1941), 25-37.

14. *Partisan Review*, VIII (November-December, 1941), 442-51.

15. "On the Brooks-MacLeish Thesis," *Partisan Review*, IX (January-February 1942), 38-47.

16. Eliot's "Letter to the Editors" appeared in *Partisan Review*, IX (March-April, 1942), 115-16.

17. Louise Bogan's "counterstatement" in *Partisan Review*, IX (January-February, 1942), 41.

18. As Eliot's name became, and largely remained so, an eidolon of negation for Brooks, so Brooks's name performed service as a bludgeon in the critical reviews of these years, 1940, 1941, 1942, often quite gratuitously. See, for instance, the *Southern Review*, VI (1940-41), and its "counterstatements" to the Philosophical Society's Symposium in 1940; Lionel Trilling's "The Sense of the Past," *Partisan Review*, IX (May-June, 1942), 240; F. O. Matthiessen, reviewing Ferner Nuhn's *The Wind Blew from the East* and Maxwell Geismar's *Writers in Crisis*, in *Partisan Review*, IX (September-October, 1942), 422.

Chapter Nine

1. See Gladys Brooks, *If Strangers Meet* (New York, 1967), a book of reminiscence of her married years with Brooks, supplementing Brooks's memoirs.

2. Letters, Brooks to Wheelock, April 12, 1956, and May 1, 1956. Quoted with permission.

3. Mary M. Colum, "Tradition, Optimism and Mr. Brooks," New York *Times Book Review*, March 29, 1953, pp. 7, 21.

4. See, for instance, *Start With the Sun: Studies in the Whitman Tradition* (University of Nebraska, 1960) by James E. Miller, Karl Shapiro, and Bernice Slote, especially the introductory essay. Also, Karl Shapiro's *In Defence of Ignorance* (New York, 1960).

5. Granville Hicks, "The Writer as Hero," *Saturday Review of Literature*, September 2, 1961, p. 18.

6. I adapt the phrase from R. P. Blackmur's review of *The Flowering of New England:* "A Prophecy of Possibilities," *Nation*, CXLIII (August 22, 1936), 218-19.

7. Irving Howe, "Modern Criticism: Privileges and Perils," in *Modern Literary Criticism: An Anthology*, ed. Howe (New York, 1961), p. 10.

8. Edmund Wilson, *The Bit Between My Teeth* (New York, 1965), p. 554.

Selected Bibliography

PRIMARY SOURCES

1. *Separate Works by Van Wyck Brooks*

These are listed in the order of their publication as separate works, though parts of many of them appeared earlier in periodicals or other people's books.

Verses by Two Undergraduates. With John Hall Wheelock. Cambridge. Privately printed, 1905.

The Wine of the Puritans: A Study of Present Day America. London: Sisley's, 1908; New York: Mitchell Kennerley, 1909.

The Soul: An Essay Towards a Point of View. San Francisco: Privately printed, 1910.

The Malady of the Ideal: Obermann, Maurice de Guerin and Amiel. London: A. C. Fifield, 1913. First American edition, with Preface by Robert E. Spiller, Philadelphia: University of Pennsylvania Press, 1947.

John Addington Symonds: A Biographical Study. New York: Mitchell Kennerley, 1914.

The World of H. G. Wells. New York: Mitchell Kennerley, 1915.

America's Coming-of-Age. New York: B. W. Huebsch, 1915.

Letters and Leadership. New York: B. W. Huebsch, 1918.

The Ordeal of Mark Twain. New York: E. P. Dutton, 1920. New and revised edition, New York: E. P. Dutton, 1933. Reprinted, with Introduction by Malcolm Cowley, New York: Meridian Books, 1955.

The Pilgrimage of Henry James. New York: E. P. Dutton, 1925.

Emerson and Others. New York: E. P. Dutton, 1927.

Sketches in Criticism. New York: E. P. Dutton, 1932.

The Life of Emerson. New York: E. P. Dutton, 1932.

Three Essays on America. New York: E. P. Dutton, 1934. Brings together *America's Coming-of-Age, Letters and Leadership,* and "The Literary Life in America," with a new preface. Reprinted as *America's Coming-of-Age,* New York: Doubleday Anchor Books, 1958.

The Flowering of New England. New York: E. P. Dutton, 1936.

New England: Indian Summer: 1865-1915. New York: E. P. Dutton, 1940.

On Literature Today. New York: E. P. Dutton, 1941.

Opinions of Oliver Allston. New York: E. P. Dutton, 1941.

The World of Washington Irving. New York: E. P. Dutton, 1944.

The Times of Melville and Whitman. New York: E. P. Dutton, 1947.

A Chilmark Miscellany. New York: E. P. Dutton, 1948.

The Confident Years: 1885-1915. New York: E. P. Dutton, 1952.

Makers and Finders: A History of the Writer in America, 1800-1915. General title of the series of five volumes: I. *The World of Washington Irving.* New York: E. P. Dutton, 1950; II. *The Flowering of New England.* New York: E. P. Dutton, 1952; III. *The Times of Melville and Whitman.* New York: E. P. Dutton, 1953; IV. *New England: Indian Summer.* New York: E. P. Dutton, 1950; V. *The Confident Years: 1885-1915.* New York: E. P. Dutton, 1955. Uniform volumes in Dutton's Everyman Series.

The Writer in America. New York: E. P. Dutton, 1953.

Scenes and Portraits: Memories of Childhood and Youth. New York: E. P. Dutton, 1954. First volume of memoirs.

John Sloan: A Painter's Life. New York: E. P. Dutton, 1955.

Helen Keller: Sketch for a Portrait. New York: E. P. Dutton, 1956.

Days of the Phoenix: The Nineteen Twenties I Remember. New York: E. P. Dutton, 1957. Second volume of memoirs.

From a Writer's Notebook. New York: E. P. Dutton, 1958.

The Dream of Arcadia: American Writers and Artists in Italy, 1760-1915. New York: E. P. Dutton, 1958.

Howells: His Life and World. New York: E. P. Dutton, 1959.

From the Shadow of the Mountain: My Post-Meridian Years. New York: E. P. Dutton, 1961. Third and final volume of memoirs.

Fenollosa and His Circle, with Other Essays in Biography. New York: E. P. Dutton, 1962.

An Autobiography. Foreword by John Hall Wheelock. Introduction by Malcolm Cowley. New York: E. P. Dutton, 1965. [The three volumes of memoirs in one.]

2. Van Wyck Brooks as Editor

On the editorial board of the *Seven Arts,* a monthly, appearing between November, 1916, and October, 1917. Brooks collected his contributions in *Letters and Leadership,* 1918.

As Associate Editor of the *Freeman,* a weekly, 1920-1924. Except for a brief period while he was on leave (from May 22, 1922, through January 10, 1923) Brooks wrote the unsigned column, "A Reviewer's Notebook," and contributed other essays and reviews. Many of his *Freeman* pieces were collected and published in *Sketches in Criticism,* 1932.

RANDOLPH BOURNE. *The History of a Literary Radical.* New York: B. W. Huebsch, 1920. Edited and with an Introduction by Brooks.

The American Caravan, A Yearbook of American Literature. New York: Macauley, 1927. Edited with Lewis Mumford, Alfred Kreymborg, and Paul Rosenfeld.

The Journal of Gamaliel Bradford, 1883-1932. Boston and New York: Houghton Mifflin Co., 1933. Edited by Brooks.

LLEWELYN POWYS. *Earth Memories.* New York: W. W. Norton, 1938. Introduction by Brooks.

CONSTANCE ROURKE. *The Roots of American Culture and Other Essays.* New York: Harcourt Brace and Co., 1942. Edited and with a Preface by Brooks.

Our Literary Heritage: A Pictorial History of the Writer in America. Photos by Otto L. Bettman. New York: E. P. Dutton, 1956. Captions and accompanying comment from *Makers and Finders.*

As General Editor of "Premier Classics of American Realism," Fawcett Publications, Brooks wrote introductory essays for the following:

HENRY ADAMS. *Democracy.* New York: Fawcett, 1961.

STEPHEN CRANE. *Maggie: A Girl of the Streets.* New York: Fawcett, 1960.

HAMLIN GARLAND. *Main-Travelled Roads.* New York: Fawcett, 1961.

HAROLD FREDERIC. *The Damnation of Theron Ware.* New York: Fawcett, 1961.

LAFCADIO HEARN. *Chita: A Memory of Lost Island.* New York: Fawcett, 1961.

ROBERT HERRICK. *Together.* New York: Fawcett, 1962.

WILLIAM DEAN HOWELLS. *Their Wedding Journey.* New York: Fawcett, 1960.

He wrote introductory essays for the following:

The American Romantics, 1800-1860: American Literature Survey. New York: Viking Portable Library, Viking Press, 1962.

Farmers and Daughters. Collected Stories of William Carlos Williams. New York: New Directions, 1962.

A New England Reader. Boston: Atheneum, 1962.

The Reader's Encyclopedia of American Literature, ed. Max J. Herzberg. New York: Thomas Y. Crowell Co., 1962.

Writers at Work: The Paris Review Interviews. New York: Viking Press, 1963.

3. Shorter Writings by Brooks

Most of Brooks's important magazine contributions—to the *Forum, Seven Arts, Freeman, Dial, New Republic, Yale Review, Harper's, Atlantic Monthly, Saturday Review of Literature*—were frequently advance appearances of parts of books in preparation, or were subsequently collected and are available in book-publications. An important exception is his essay, "On Creating a Usable Past," *Dial,* LXIV (April 11, 1918), 337-41. The first appearance of "The Literary Life in America" in *Civilization in the United States: An Inquiry by Thirty Americans,* edited by Harold Stearns (New York, 1922), ought to be noted for the importance of the historical context provided by its companion inquiries. Two poems and a short sketch written by

Brooks as an undergraduate for the Harvard *Advocate* are reprinted in *The Harvard Advocate Anthology,* ed. Donald Hall (New York: Twayne Publishers, 1950), pp. 87-92.

4. *Letters*

The Library of the University of Pennsylvania has a significant Brooks collection, including Brooks's own files of correspondence. Much of his correspondence, however, remains uncollected and very little has been published, although a volume of letters is in preparation. Four of his letters were included by Upton Sinclair in the latter's *My Lifetime in Letters* (Columbia: University of Missouri Press, 1960). See also Sherwood Anderson's "Letters to Van Wyck Brooks," *Story* (September-October, 1941), 19-62, reprinted in Edmund Wilson (ed.), *The Shock of Recognition* (New York: Farrar, Straus and Cudahy, 1955). For Randolph Bourne's letters to Brooks, see Louis Filler, *Randolph Bourne* (Washington, D.C.: American Council of Public Affairs, 1943); Lillian Schlissel (ed.), *The World of Randolph Bourne* (New York: E. P. Dutton, 1965). Also, John Hall Wheelock (ed.), *Editor to Author: The Letters of Maxwell Perkins* (New York: Charles Scribner's Sons, 1950).

SECONDARY SOURCES

1. *Bibliographies and Checklists*

Few checklists of Brooks's work were able to keep up with his productivity and are consequently largely incomplete and out of date. Fred B. Millett, *Contemporary American Authors* (New York: Harcourt, Brace and Company, 1940), and the volume in Bibliography of the *Literary History of the United States,* edited by Robert E. Spiller and others, along with the Bibliography's *Supplement,* edited by Richard M. Ludwig (New York: Macmillan Company, 1959), are useful for their references to secondary materials and listings of reprinted editions of Brooks's work. For secondary sources see also Lewis Leary (ed.), *Articles on American Literature, 1900-1950* (Durham, N. C.: Duke University Press, 1954).

2. *Some General Studies with Parts Devoted to Van Wyck Brooks*

A. Early estimates

BEACH, JOSEPH WARREN. "Van Wyck Brooks: Scientific Jargon," *The Outlook for American Prose.* Chicago: University of Chicago Press, 1926. Early attempt to locate Brooks's shortcomings in his style. Brief, but suggestive.

DE VOTO, BERNARD. *Mark Twain's America.* Boston: Little, Brown & Co., 1932. See Chapter IX, "The Critics of Mark Twain." Important critique of *The Ordeal of Mark Twain* and Brooks's failure to understand the West.

FOERSTER, NORMAN. *Toward Standards: A Study of the Present Critical Movement in American Letters.* New York: Farrar & Rinehart, 1930. Good assessment of the differences between the humanists and "The Literary Prophets"—Brooks, Bourne, *et al.*

FRANK, WALDO. *Our America.* New York: Boni & Liveright, 1919. Literary prophecy in apocalyptic prose. Strong on the Puritan and the pioneer. Tribute to Brooks's role as liberator.

ROSENFELD, PAUL. "Van Wyck Brooks," *Port of New York: Essays on Fourteen Modern Americans.* New York: Harcourt, Brace & Co., 1924. The best of the early judgments of Brooks as a critic.

B. Later estimates and studies (since the 1930's)

AARON, DANIEL. *Writers on the Left.* New York: Harcourt, Brace & World, Inc., 1961. Excellent account of the mixture of politics and literature. Brooks's role during both his early and later phases (into the 1930's) given comment, and judicious assessment.

BROOKS, GLADYS. *If Strangers Meet: A Memory.* New York: Harcourt, Brace & World, Inc., 1967. Supplements Brooks's memoirs.

COWLEY, MALCOLM. *Exile's Return.* New York: Viking Press, 1934, 1951. A literary odyssey of the period of Brooks's influence.

DE VOTO, BERNARD. *The Literary Fallacy.* Boston: Little, Brown & Co., 1944. Brooks singled out as the most intelligent exponent of "the literary fallacy." The most extended and severe critique of Brooks to date.

FORCEY, CHARLES. *The Crossroads of Liberalism.* New York: Oxford University Press, 1961. Good on the relationship of Brooks and Bourne and the *New Republic* leadership of the Progressive era.

FRAIBERG, LOUIS. "Van Wyck Brooks versus Mark Twain versus Samuel Clemens," *Psychoanalysis and American Literary Criticism.* Detroit: Wayne State University Press, 1960. An examination of Brooks's use of psychoanalytical concepts and terms in *The Ordeal of Mark Twain.* Thorough in its study of that book but does not probe beyond it to define Brooks's uses of psychology in a broader sense.

HOFFMAN, FREDERICK J. *The Twenties: American Writing in the Postwar Decade.* New, revised edition. New York: Collier Books, 1962. Good attention to Brooks, Mencken, *et al.* in the attack on Puritanism and the uses of the past.

HOWE, IRVING. "Introduction—Modern Criticism: Privileges and Perils," *Modern Literary Criticism.* New York: Grove Press, Inc., 1961. This collection of critical essays edited by Howe includes no selections by Brooks, but the introductory essay is one of the best short surveys of the critical movements Brooks influenced or reacted to that I have read.

HYMAN, STANLEY EDGAR. "Van Wyck Brooks and Biographical Criticism," *The Armed Vision: A Study in the Methods of Modern Criticism*. New York: Alfred A. Knopf, 1948. Hard-hitting criticism of the shortcomings of Brooks's method, judged successful only in *The Ordeal of Mark Twain*. Marred by some hasty inferences.

KAZIN, ALFRED. *On Native Grounds*. New York: Harcourt, Brace & Co., 1942. Noting "reversal," but sensitive to the claims of both phases of Brooks's career.

LEARY, LEWIS. "Introduction: Standing with Reluctant Feet," *A Casebook on Mark Twain's Wound*. New York: Thomas Y. Crowell Co., 1962. Excellent summary review of the controversy over *The Ordeal of Mark Twain* with most of the important documents provided in the Casebook that follows.

MATTHIESSEN, F. O. *The Responsibilities of the Critic:* Essays and Reviews by F. O. Matthiessen, selected by John Rackliffe. New York: Oxford University Press, 1952. Reprints Matthiessen's reviews of *The Flowering of New England* and *The World of Washington Irving*, both essays extended examinations of the results of Brooks's method—as an abandonment of the critic's tools of analysis in favor of evoking personality.

MAY, HENRY F. *The End of American Innocence: The First Years of Our Own Time, 1912-1917*. New York: Alfred A. Knopf, 1959. Good on the intellectual and cultural currents that gave Brooks's early work its force.

PRITCHARD, JOHN PAUL. *Criticism in America*. Norman: University of Oklahoma Press, 1956. Brief survey of Brooks's later phase, of the "spleen" in his attack on the New Critics.

RALEIGH, JOHN H. "Revolt and Revaluation in Criticism: 1900-1930," *The Development of American Literary Criticism*, ed. Floyd Stovall. Chapel Hill: University of North Carolina Press, 1955. Objective survey of what the criticism of the period accomplished.

SMITH, BERNARD. *Forces in American Criticism*. New York: Harcourt, Brace & Co., 1939. Marxist in emphasis. Treats Brooks in the war of traditions, covering his work through *The Flowering of New England*.

SPILLER, ROBERT E. "The Battle of the Books," in *The Literary History of the United States*, ed. Spiller *et al.*, Vol. II. New York: Macmillan, 1948. Emphasis upon Brooks's literary radicalism.

————. "Literature and the Critics," *American Perspectives*, ed. Spiller and Eric Larrabee. Cambridge: Harvard University Press, 1961.

————. "The Critical Rediscovery of America," *A Time of Harvest,* ed. Spiller. New York: Hill & Wang, 1962. Both emphasize Brooks's earlier phase.

SUTTON, WALTER. *Modern American Criticism.* Englewood Cliffs, N. J.: Prentice-Hall, Inc., 1963. Brief discussion of *The Ordeal of Mark Twain* as an early but not serious application of Freud, and of Brooks's early work as a contribution to liberal literary criticism.

TURNER, SUSAN J. *A History of the Freeman: Literary Landmark of the Early Twenties.* New York and London: Columbia University Press, 1963. Model study. Brooks figures prominently.

WASSERSTROM, WILLIAM. *The Time of the Dial.* Syracuse, N. Y.: Syracuse University Press, 1963. Somewhat thesis-ridden, but provocative; useful for emphasis upon relations between Brooks and the esthetic *Dial.*

WILSON, EDMUND. *Classics and Commercials: A Literary Chronicle of the Forties.* New York: Farrar, Straus, 1950.

————. *The Shores of Light: A Literary Chronicle of the Twenties and Thirties.* New York: Farrar, Straus & Young, 1952.

————. *The Bit Between My Teeth: A Literary Chronicle of 1950-1965.* New York: Farrar, Straus & Giroux, 1965. All three volumes reprint Wilson's several reviews and essays on Brooks, revealing steadily mounting respect. For Wilson's views on Brooks and the "coldness of the academics" toward him, see the essay "Newton Arvin's *Longfellow*" in the last volume.

3. Critical Articles

A. Early reviews and estimates (before 1936)

ARVIN, NEWTON. "Books," *Commonweal,* II (May 6, 1925), 719-20. Favorable summary review of Brooks's work up to and including *The Pilgrimage of Henry James.*

BURKE, KENNETH. "Van Wyck Brooks in Transition?," *Dial,* LXXXIV (January, 1928), 56-59. Review, *Emerson and Others,* speculating whether essay on Melville, where art for once is not explained by Brooks as a "social result," marks a shift in Brooks's criticism.

CHAMBERLAIN, JOHN. "Van Wyck Brooks," *New Freeman,* I (June 11, 1930), 299-301. Defense of Brooks from attack by the humanists.

COLLINS, SEWARD. "Criticism in America: The Origins of a Myth," *Bookman,* LXX (June, 1930), 241-56; 353-64. Critique of the anti-Puritan thesis in Brooks and his followers.

DONLIN, GEORGE. "The Impotence of American Culture," *Dial,* LXV (September 19, 1918), 205-7. Review of *Letters and Leadership* noting symbolic force of Brooks's portrait of America.

GLICKSBURG, CHARLES I. "Van Wyck Brooks," *Sewanee Review*, XLIII (April-June, 1935), 175-86. Review of *Three Essays on America*.

GREGORY, ALŸSE. "A Superb Brief," *Dial*, LXXIX (September, 1925), 235-38. Review of *The Pilgrimage of Henry James*.

HACKETT, FRANCIS. "Creative America," *New Republic*, XVI (September 28, 1918), 261-62. Review of *Letters and Leadership*, finding it morose, but true.

JONES, HOWARD MUMFORD. "The Pilgrimage of Van Wyck Brooks," *Virginia Quarterly Review*, VIII (July, 1932), 439-42. Review of *The Life of Emerson* as "aesthetic creation" rather than historical reconstruction.

KENTON, EDNA. "Henry James and Mr. Van Wyck Brooks," *Bookman*, LXII (October, 1925), 152-57. Highly critical of Brooks's method of paraphrase.

LIPPMANN, WALTER. "Isaiah, Jr.," *New Republic*, V (January 1, 1916), 229-30. Review of *America's Coming-of-Age*.

MUNSON, GORHAM B. "Van Wyck Brooks: His Sphere and His Encroachments," *Dial*, LXXVIII (January, 1925), 28-42. Review and analysis of Brooks's ideas and style to explain his leadership in creating a "way of thinking about literature." See Munson's later review of "The Young Critics of the Nineteen-Twenties," *Bookman*, LXX (December, 1929), 369-73.

OPPENHEIM, JAMES. "The Story of the Seven Arts," *American Mercury*, XX (June, 1930), 156-64. Credits Brooks's leadership.

SHERMAN, STUART P. "The Battle of the Brows," *Nation*, CII (February 17, 1916), 196-97. Mocking review of *America's Coming-of Age*.

SPILLER, ROBERT E. "Militant Criticism," *Saturday Review of Literature*, IX (January 21, 1933), 386. Review of *Sketches in Criticism* finding these essays of a decade before out of date, largely negative, with only a vague hypothesis of affirmation.

B. Later reviews and estimates (after 1936)

AIKEN, CONRAD. "American Writers Come of Age," *Atlantic Monthly*, CLXIX (April, 1942), 476-81. Takes strong issue with *Opinions of Oliver Allston*. See also Brooks's "In Reply to Conrad Aiken," *Atlantic Monthly*, CLXIX (May, 1942) [after p. 665].

BAKER, CARLOS. "In the Twenties, A Coming of Age," New York *Times Book Review*, March 17, 1957, pp. 1, 45. Review of *Days of the Phoenix*.

BERTHOFF, WARNER. Review of *Dream of Arcadia*, in *New England Quarterly*, XXXII (June, 1959), 251-53. Prefers Brooks's memoirs and *John Sloan* as Brooks's "real contribution to our literature," the dream of an ideal community of artists being more rightly proportioned in those books.

CARGILL, OSCAR. "The Ordeal of Van Wyck Brooks," *College English,* VIII (November, 1946), 55-61. Emphasis on reviewer response to Brooks's work from *Wine of the Puritans* to *The World of Washington Irving.* Vernon Lee suggested as influence on Brooks's aims as a critic.

CHASE, RICHARD. "New vs. Ordealist," *Kenyon Review,* XI (Winter, 1949), 11-13. Part of symposium on the New Criticism. Brief but suggestive contrast with the school Brooks set in motion.

COLUM, MARY M. "Tradition, Optimism, and Mr. Brooks," New York *Times Book Review,* March 29, 1953, pp. 7, 21. Review of *The Writer in America.*

COWLEY, MALCOLM. "Mr. Brooks Dissenting," *New Republic,* CV (November 24, 1941), 705-6; CV (December 1, 1941), 738-39. On *Opinions of Oliver Allston.*

————. "Van Wyck Brooks' Great Evocation of Our Literary Past," New York *Herald-Tribune Book Review,* January 6, 1952, pp. 1, 27. Review of *The Confident Years.*

————. "Brooks' Mark Twain: Thirty-Five Years After," *New Republic,* CXXXII (June 20, 1955), 17-18. [Reprinted as Introduction to *The Ordeal of Mark Twain.* New York: Meridian Books, 1955.]

————. "Van Wyck Brooks at 75," *Saturday Review,* XLIV (February 18, 1961), 15, 73.

————. "Van Wyck Brooks: A Career in Retrospect," *Saturday Review,* XLVI (May 25, 1963), 17-18, 38. [Revised and expanded for the Introduction to Brooks's *An Autobiography.* New York: E. P. Dutton, 1965.] Like Edmund Wilson, Cowley, while frequently disagreeing with Brooks, has steadily admired his achievement for his generation.

CUNLIFFE, MARCUS. "American Expatriates," *Encounter,* XIII (July, 1959), 76-77. Review of *The Dream of Arcadia,* insisting it should have been a different book, that Brooks was not trying hard enough.

DUPEE, FREDERICK W. "The Americanism of Van Wyck Brooks," *Partisan Review,* VI (Summer, 1939), 69-85. Reprinted in *Critiques and Essays in Criticism, 1920-1948,* ed. R. W. Stallman; and also in Morton Dauwen Zabel (ed.), *Literary Opinion in America.* One of the best appraisals.

HICKS, GRANVILLE. "The Writer as Hero," *Saturday Review,* XLIV (September 2, 1961), 12. Review of *From the Shadow of the Mountain.*

HOWE, IRVING. "The Gentility of Van Wyck Brooks," *New Republic,* CXLI (November 9, 1959), 21-22. Review of *Howells.* Restates nearly all the complaints against Brooks's later phase.

MACDONALD, DWIGHT. "Kulturbolschewismus is Here," *Partisan Re-*

view, VIII (November-December, 1941), 442-51. See also: "On the Brooks-MacLeish Thesis," *Partisan Review*, IX (January-February, 1942), 38-47. (Allen Tate, William Carlos Williams, Henry Miller, Louise Bogan, James T. Farrell, Lionel Trilling.) Part of the controversy over *Opinions of Oliver Allston*.

MUMFORD, LEWIS. "Our Rich Vein of Literary Ore," *Saturday Review*, XXX (November 8, 1947), 11-13. Review of *The Times of Melville and Whitman*.

SPILLER, ROBERT E. "What Became of the Literary Radicals?," *New Republic*, CXV (November 18, 1946), 664-66.

––––––. "Pageant of Literary America," *Saturday Review*, XXXV (January 5, 1952), 11-12. Review of *The Confident Years*.

TRILLING, LIONEL. "A Young Critic in a Younger America," New York *Times Book Review*, March 7, 1954, 1, 28. Review of *Scenes and Portraits* and Brooks's decline as a critic.

WEIMER, DAVID R. "Anxiety in the Golden Day of Lewis Mumford," *New England Quarterly*, XXXVI (June, 1963), 172-91. Relations between Brooks and Mumford; suggests Matthew Arnold as a strong influence on Brooks.

WHEELOCK, JOHN HALL. "Dear Men and Women" (In Memory of Van Wyck Brooks), *New Yorker*, XXXIX (July 13, 1963), 22. A poem, reprinted in Wheelock's "Foreword" to Brooks's *An Autobiography*. New York: E. P. Dutton, 1965.

The following two important items appeared after this book had been completed and submitted to the printer:

SPRAGUE, CLAIRE (ed.). *Van Wyck Brooks: The Early Years, A Selection From His Works, 1908-1921*. New York: Harper Torchbooks, Harper & Row, 1968. Includes *The Wine of the Puritans* complete, selections from *The Soul*, the original 1915 edition of *America's Coming-of-Age*, six of the *Seven Arts* essays, two *Dial* essays including "On Creating a Usable Past," and four *Freeman* essays. Introduction and Notes.

WASSERSTROM, WILLIAM. *Van Wyck Brooks*. Minneapolis: University of Minnesota Pamphlets on American Writers, No. 71, 1968. Argues that Brooks exploited Bernard Hart's *The Psychology of Insanity* "lock, stock, and barrel." A speculative venture into the "psychology of motive" in Brooks's work.

Index